The Indwelling

An Introduction to a New Relationship with God

The Indwelling

An Introduction to a New Relationship with God

James Cardona

1st EDITION

Publishing by James Cardona

Printing by LULU.COM

I wish to thank my wife, Majdalin Cardona, for her support.

I also wish to thank Richard and Maria Sanchez for their help in this work.

I wish to thank Richard Hitchon for his valuable contributions of reviewing and editing this book for content and accuracy and for praying with me.

The following quoted works are used with permission from their respective copyright holders:
Franklin Institute Weather Graphs © by The Franklin Institute.
McGrath, Alister, *Reformation Thought* © by Blackwell Publishing.
Nebula image in cover art courtesy of NASA/ JPL- Caltech.

The Indwelling:
An Introduction to a New Relationship with God

ISBN: 978-0-6151-3668-4

Printed in the United States of America

CONTENTS

INTRODUCTION

his book is a collection of essays written over a period of several years. The essays are only related in terms of subject. They all have to do with Jesus, Christianity, and the relationship of the Christian to God. Each essay may not necessarily be dependent upon any other and can be read in any order. Likewise, they are not listed in order of the time of their writing, significance, or importance but only in an arbitrary order of my own choosing. This collection of essays has different topics but several of the essays have to do with the indwelling of the Holy Spirit, hence the title of the book.

Intended Audience

The intended audience of most of these essays is someone who is already a believer in the gospel message. For example, I do not dwell heavily on the doctrine of justification because I already assume that the reader believes. To be justified is to be made righteous in the eyes of God, to have accepted the gift of righteousness God gives when you step forward and say that you believe. I assume that the reader has already done this. This work is introductory though, it does not dwell too heavily in complex and deep subjects, but tries to provide practical and useful information that believers can put into practice and use with results.

Assumptions

This book makes the assumption that the reader believes the Bible to be the true Word of God. That is, that the Bible can be quoted as authoritative and absolute. Whenever there is a question concerning doctrine, the answer is always determined by the Bible.

A second assumption I make is that the reader believes that every promise of the Bible is available for the contemporary Christian. Any promise in the Bible that was given "to all people" is available "to all people" today.

I use the term "assumption" only to mean that I do not prove those things in this book. I believe them completely and I *assume* that the reader believes them also; therefore I do not prove them.

Where Did This Come From?

These essays came about in a peculiar way. For many years I read the Bible, I read commentaries on the Bible, I went to church and sat attentive, listening to what the pastor or priest said, but it seemed I could not keep all the various doctrines straight. I found in my study that I had contradictory beliefs that I could not prove using the Bible.

I decided to write down everything I believed. Then, whenever I came across a scripture that either proved or disproved those beliefs I would edit my writings. All doctrine must be supported by the Bible and no doctrine should make one scripture trump another. All scripture must be in agreement or the doctrine is incorrect. Of course, the Holy Spirit has been leading me in what He would have me to know, and therefore my writings only cover a limited range of topics. I only know what the Holy Spirit has shown me and nothing more. The essays found in this book are based on some of those original writings.

References and Typeface

References from the Bible have been taken from a variety of versions based solely on conveying the meaning most easily. But, almost all references are from the *King James Version.* In a few select cases I have used other versions only because the wording was a bit easier to understand. The meaning was not any different, only worded a little better. There are references to other works also. Most all of the essays or sermon transcripts of Luther, Calvin, Zwingli, Erasmus, Wesley, Branham and others should be found freely and easily on the web, so you should not have to buy any books to gain access to the primary source.

I have used the following system in this book. Words that are spoken or thought are in italics. Additionally, words spoken by God, Jesus, or any prophet who uses *"Thus saith the Lord"* are in *a **special font that looks like this.*** I liberally use bold, caps, and italics for emphasis, even in Bible quotes.

Limitations

I have attempted to limit these essays in that the scope of each is to answer only a question or two. I find that if a person tries to cover an entire subject that it is rarely done full justice. I would never buy a book that has, *Everything you always wanted to know about…* or *The complete…* in its title because I do not believe it is possible to cover any subject completely in one book. But there is a different liability in my method. I may be generating more questions and confusion than help, so in some cases there are later essays to expand on foundational material in earlier ones. This is the best I can do. Understand that these were only written as educational for me, originally, and I might not explain the things that I already knew at the time of the writing.

Supported by the Word and Spirit

I know that many people like to make authoritative sounding statements, attach a few scriptures to them and then it becomes a doctrine. Later, others read it without proving it through the scripture and being led of the Spirit of God. Now that is exactly how people become misled.

4

I realize that the things that I say or write will be held against me on the Day of Judgment, and I know if I *don't* say or write them it will be held against me on the Day of Judgment. We cannot bury the coin that is given us by God. So I am trying to be as honest, truthful, and sincere as I can.

Disagreements

No doubt there'll be many who disagree with sections of this writing, but I want to prove it by the scriptures of the Bible. If you disagree then please first read the whole essay, take the scriptures, study them and pray and see if the Lord doesn't prove it to be right –ask the Lord to reveal it to you. All doctrine must be supported by the Word in every way and in every angle. If you find me in error, then it is your responsibility to correct me using the Word.

If you happen to be thoroughly set in your doctrine and you disagree with what I wrote then understand that I am not condemning your doctrine, I am just expressing what the Lord has shown me. Now, I have met people that can read a book and the first time they come across something they disagree with, they set it down. Even if they are on page one, they stop reading. I hope that people do not do that with this book. As I said, it covers a variety of topics and if you find one you disagree with, perhaps you can pass by that one and continue on. It has been famously said that a person does not throw away a whole cherry pie just because they found one seed. They throw away the seed and keep eating!

Cost and Commission

This book has been printed at minimum cost with no one, including the publisher or the printing company, taking a commission. If you have come across this book and would like a copy, but cannot afford it, then I urge you to download a free copy from the internet. Go to the printer's website: www.lulu.com and search under my name or the book title. It does not matter to me if you buy a printed copy or download the free one because, as I said, I make NOTHING from its sale.

True Stories

There are several true personal stories in this book. I want to say that these are not fiction or exaggerations. These events truly happened exactly how I state them. God does not need me to exaggerate for Him.

Additionally, I do not place these stories in this book to say, *"Look what I did!"* These stories are for God's glory, not mine. I only happened to be there or to be involved, but it was God's power all the time doing the works.

God is real. These experiences with God are real. God operates today the same as He did back in the days of the prophets and back in the days of the apostles. I am nobody special, you can have an experience with God too.

Purpose

The purpose of most of these essays is to give the Christian who reads them a fuller understanding of the gospel and to perhaps cause people to re-evaluate their relationship with God, hopefully making them grow closer. In some cases, I am only trying to raise questions in people's minds so they might desire to study more.

This book has a practical nature. Its purpose is to provide useful information that can help you. It does not talk about things that will happen far off in the future, maybe one thousand years from now. It does not talk about things that happened one thousand years ago, unless they can be used as an example to help us today. This book talks about things that can help you right now, today. This book talks about things that will affect your life and change you right now, drawing you closer to God.

The purpose of this book is not to push incorrect doctrine. Of course, I have been wrong before, but a far worse crime is to know you are wrong and not change. We, as Americans, have the right to argue as hard as we can for what we believe in and if tomorrow we find out we were wrong, we should argue tomorrow as hard as we can for the opposing view. So, with all sincerity, I am writing what I believe to be the truth. If I am wrong, I want to know. Feel free to show me my error, but show me using the Word of God.

The purpose of this book is not to place myself in authority over anyone else, simply because I wrote a book or because the Lord has revealed something to me. The purpose of this book is not to puff up. I am not a teacher. I am not a theologian. I am just a guy who prays for people and loves the Lord.

My purpose is to share what I have learned in hope that it might help someone. If it has reached your hands then I hope it is a blessing to you.[1]

---

[1] Some portions of this introduction may be repeated in the beginning of some chapters because I wanted to ensure that certain points were emphasized to the reader if they received a copy of only one chapter.

One

SIN AND FAITH

f asked, "What is sin," most people would answer with an example of a sin, saying, "A sin is disobeying your father and mother, murder, or stealing." But these are only types of sin. Asked to be more exact, a Christian might say, "A sin is disobeying one of the laws of God as written in the Bible." This definition is also limited because it looks only at exterior physical action and not at what is inside a person. Actually, this flawed definition of sin is exactly what the priests of Jesus' time thought. Regardless if they were called Pharisees, Sadducees, scribes, lawyers, or high priests in the various passages in the Bible, Jesus scolded them. In Matthew 15: 1-11, it says:

> Then some Pharisees and teachers of the law came to Jesus from Jerusalem and asked, "Why do your disciples break the tradition of the elders?

9

They don't wash their hands before they eat!"

Jesus replied, *"And why do you break the command of God for the sake of your tradition?*

For God said, Honor your father and mother and anyone who curses his father or mother must be put to death.

But you say that if a man says to his father or mother, 'Whatever help you might otherwise have received from me is a gift devoted to God,' he is not to honor his father with it.

Thus you nullify the word of God for the sake of your tradition.

You hypocrites! Isaiah was right when he prophesied about you:

'These people honor Me with their lips, but their hearts are far from Me.

They worship Me in vain; their teachings are but rules taught by men.'"

Jesus called the crowd to Him and said, **"Listen and understand.**

What goes into a man's mouth does not make him unclean, but what comes out of his mouth, that is what makes him unclean."

Sin is a Symptom of Unbelief

The priests obeyed the letter of the law but did not obey the *intent* of the law. They did not have faith in God in their hearts but because they *physically* obeyed the law they thought themselves to be righteous. Jesus said they were still condemned.

In Matthew 23:23-24, 26-28, Jesus says:
> *Woe to you, teachers of the law and Pharisees, you hypocrites!*
>
> *You give a tenth of your spices—mint, dill and cumin.*
>
> *But you have neglected the more important matters of the law —justice, mercy and faithfulness.*
>
> *You should have practiced the latter, without neglecting the former. You blind guides!*
>
> *You clean the outside of the cup and dish, but inside they are full of greed and self-indulgence.*
>
> *Blind Pharisee!* **First clean the inside of the cup and dish, and then the outside also will be clean.**
>
> *Woe to you, teachers of the law and Pharisees, you hypocrites!*
>
> *You are like whitewashed tombs, which look beautiful on the outside but on the inside are full of dead men's bones and everything unclean.*

*In the same way, on the outside you appear
to people as righteous but on the inside you
are full of hypocrisy and wickedness.*

Sickness

In Romans 14:23, it is written, "…everything that does not come from faith is sin." Let me give you an analogy to better understand this. When a person has a sickness, a head cold for example, they have some symptoms associated with the sickness. In the case of the head cold, their sinuses might be stuffy and maybe they cannot breathe through their nose. They might have a headache. Sometimes they will have body aches, tiredness, or coughs. These are the symptoms of the sickness, but they are not the sickness itself. The sickness itself is a bacterium that is inside the human body.

Likewise, sins are "symptoms" of unbelief in God's promise. Because someone does not *truly* believe God, that person has a spiritual "disease" of unbelief in the heart. The sickness of unbelief manifests itself in physical symptoms such as lying, cheating, and stealing. Like a cold, these sins are outward signs of an inward condition. In the case of the cold it is a bacteria, in the case of sin it is a lack of faith. Jesus said in Matthew 15:18-20:

*Don't you see that whatever enters the
mouth goes into the stomach and then out of
the body?*
*But the things that come out of the mouth
come from the heart, and these make a man
unclean.*

> *For out of the heart come evil thoughts,*
> *murder, adultery, sexual immorality, theft,*
> *false testimony, slander.*
> *These are what make a man unclean; but*
> *eating with unwashed hands does not make*
> *him unclean.*

And in Luke 6:45, Jesus says:

> *The good man brings good things out of*
> *the good stored up in his heart, and the evil*
> *man brings evil things out of the evil stored up*
> *in his heart. For out of the overflow of his*
> *heart his mouth speaks.*

Good Works are a Symptom of Faith

Now let us look at the inverse side. If a *lack* of faith inside a person produces the outward symptoms of sin, then what are the outward physical "symptoms" of a person *full* of faith? If you are full of faith internally, there will be external evidence. Jesus speaks to the priests about how good works are a result of an inward condition in Matthew 12:33-35:

> *Make a tree good and its fruit will be good,*
> *or make a tree bad and its fruit will be bad,*
> *for a tree is recognized by its fruit.*
> *You brood of vipers, how can you who are*
> *evil say anything good?*
> *For out of the overflow of the heart the*
> *mouth speaks.*

> *The good man brings good things out of the good stored up in him, and the evil man brings evil things out of the evil stored up in him.*

So then, what are good works? In Matthew 6:1-2 it is written that giving to the needy is a good work. But in both Mark 14 and John 12, a woman uses expensive oil to anoint Jesus instead of selling it to give money to the poor. Jesus says this is her good work. It is wrong to think that good works are only specific actions that we must do. The way we should govern our actions is to be led by the Spirit. If God is dwelling inside of you, He will tell you what works to perform.

Faith vs. Works

"Hold on a minute," you say, *"I am saved by grace! —I don't need works to get into heaven!"* I will agree with you, BUT, in James 2:14-26, it expounds on how *Faith without works is dead.* What is dead? The faith is dead. If there is a real **living** faith inside then, like the cold, there will be no choice but to display the "symptoms" of that faith and perform good works. You will not be able to stop yourself because it is what is inside of you, the Holy Spirit, that is driving you toward performing those good works.

There is a doctrine attributed to Martin Luther that states (incorrectly) that Christians do not need to do good works because they are justified (saved) by faith ALONE. In response, I tell you that once a person is justified AND the Spirit dwells within, that person WILL do good works – if not doing good works then, according to *James*, the faith inside of that person is dead.

Jesus told a parable in Luke 19:11-27 of how an owner gave a certain amount of money to three different workers to invest while he was away. One worker was given one coin, another three, and another ten. The man with one coin buried it in the ground and gave it back to the owner with no interest, while the other two men invested their coins and made a profit. The guy with one coin was *cast out into outer darkness* while the other two were given rewards. If we see this parable of three men to mean they are saved or lost and the coins as something from God such as spiritual gifts or messages, then this is a hard saying. The guy with one coin had dealings with the owner, who is Jesus, and even Jesus gave him a coin! But you see he took this gift –maybe it was the message that Jesus saves –and he buried it. He hid it from everyone. No one could even see that he was any different, so in effect, he wasn't any different. He had no works inside of him –his faith was dead. When the judgment came, he thought he was OK because he thought he had accepted Christ as his Savior. He had a relationship with the owner! He made a "mental" confession of faith –but at the judgment seat, Jesus said He didn't know him. The faith that was in his heart had died.

Higher Places in Heaven

Others hold the opposite argument, that we should do works to gain merits and a higher place in heaven. They reference verses like Matthew 6:1-2 where Jesus says:

> *Be careful not to do your acts of*
> *righteousness before men, to be seen by them.*
> *If you do, you will have **no reward**
> **from your Father in heaven.***
> *So when you give to the needy, do not*
> *announce it with trumpets, as the hypocrites*

> *do in the synagogues and on the streets, to be*
> *honored by men.*
> *I tell you the truth, they have received*
> *their reward in full.*

Again, I must agree that God in heaven recognizes good works even though they do not save us. But I must add a caveat. We do not do good works to earn points –this is wrong thinking. We do good works because the Spirit inside of us leads us to do them. Jesus said in Luke 17:7-10:

> *Suppose one of you had a servant plowing*
> *or looking after the sheep.*
> *Would he say to the servant when he comes*
> *in from the field, 'Come along now and sit*
> *down to eat?'*
> *Would he not rather say, 'Prepare my*
> *supper, get yourself ready and wait on me*
> *while I eat and drink; after that you may eat*
> *and drink?'*
> *Would he thank the servant because he did*
> *what he was told to do?*
> *So you also, when you have done*
> *everything you were told to do, should say,*
> *'We are unworthy servants; we have only*
> *done our duty.'*

It is our *duty* to do good works because the Holy Spirit inside of us commands us to do them – no more.

Ephesians 2:8-10 puts the whole controversy between grace and works in perfect balance. It says:

> **For it is by grace you have been saved,**
> through faith—and this not from yourselves, it

is the gift of God— not by works, so that no
one can boast.
   For we are God's workmanship, **created
in Christ Jesus to do good works**, which
God prepared in advance for us to do.

   In summary, we are saved by God's grace. Salvation is
what He does for us. Faith is the channel that we use to connect to
God. And *after* we are saved, good works are what we do for Him.

Symptoms Do Not Point Toward Condition,
Condition Points Toward Symptoms

   Back to our analogy of the cold, sometimes I get a sniffle
or a headache and I think, "*I feel a cold coming on,*" but it never
comes. I don't get the cold. Perhaps the sniffle or headache was
caused by something else. I had the outward physical symptoms of
a cold but did not actually have the bacteria present inside my
body.

   Likewise, with sin and faith. We find that people can be
saved, have faith in God, and want to stop sinning, but cannot
bring themselves to stop. Years of habit make quitting smoking
and other vices difficult. Typically, they *do* feel strong conviction
to stop, which is of the Holy Spirit. So for these people, there exist
the outward "symptoms" of an inward condition of a *lack* of faith.
Actually, they have some amount of faith in them, however small.
Sanctification is a process whereby the Holy Spirit convicts a
person of these sins, causing a person to start to lead a holy life,
and for some people this process can take a long period of time.

So, obtaining faith *inside* should take priority over eliminating sinful behavior *outside* because once a person gains faith inside, the sinful lifestyle will leave through sanctification. Jesus said, **"First** *clean the inside of the cup and dish, and then the outside also will be clean."* [2]

In Galatians 5: 16-18, Paul writes:

So I say, live by the Spirit, and you will not gratify the desires of the sinful nature.

For the sinful nature desires what is contrary to the Spirit, and the Spirit what is contrary to the sinful nature.

They are in conflict with each other, so that you do not do what you want.

But if you are led by the Spirit, you are not under law.

The Old Testament Israelites practiced circumcision –a cutting away of a portion of the flesh. In the New Testament, both Peter and Paul separately argue that the Holy Spirit cuts away the unwanted portion of our spirit, that *the Holy Spirit is the circumcision of the human spirit.* In Romans 2:28-29, it is written:

A man is not a Jew if he is only one outwardly, nor is circumcision merely outward and physical.

No, a man is a Jew if he is one inwardly; and **circumcision is circumcision of the heart, by the Spirit, not by the written code**.

Such a man's praise is not from men, but from God.

So, if a person can be saved and still sin, can people perform good works that are unsaved? Sure, there are many people who perform good works who have no faith. There are people full of charity, working at soup kitchens, and homeless

---

[2] Matthew 23:26

shelters, for example, who do not even know God. These people have the "symptoms" of faith without having faith. In Luke 13:22-28, the Bible records one of Jesus' Parables:

> Then Jesus went through the towns and villages, teaching as He made his way to Jerusalem. Someone asked Him, *"Lord, are only a few people going to be saved?"*
>
> He said to them, *"Make every effort to enter through the narrow door, because many, I tell you, will try to enter and will not be able to. Once the owner of the house gets up and closes the door, you will stand outside knocking and pleading, 'Sir, open the door for us.'*
>
> *But He will answer, 'I don't know you or where you come from.'*
>
> *Then you will say, '**We ate and drank with You, and You taught in our streets.'**
>
> *But He will reply, 'I don't know you or where you come from. Away from me, all you evildoers!'*
>
> *There will be weeping there, and gnashing of teeth, when you see Abraham, Isaac and Jacob and all the prophets in the kingdom of God, but you yourselves thrown out."*

These people, who were locked out of heaven, *knew* who Jesus was – they had taken communion (ate with Him) and *knew* His teachings, *yet He did not know them.* Are these people then saved? Clearly, No. They were locked out. Just as faith without works is dead, likewise works without faith is dead. I tell you that even Mother Teresa is condemned if she is relying only on her "good works" to save her. If works alone could save you then what did Jesus come for?

Also look at Matthew 7:21-23, Jesus says:
> *Not everyone who says to Me, 'Lord, Lord,' will enter the kingdom of heaven, but only he who does the will of my Father who is in heaven.*
>
> ***Many will say to Me on that day, 'Lord, Lord, did we not prophesy in Your name, and in Your name drive out demons and perform many miracles?'***
> *Then I will tell them plainly, '**I never knew you**. Away from Me, you evildoers!'*

The magnitude or type of work does not matter. It is still a work and does not save. You could perform the same works as Jesus and that work would still not save you. We are saved by faith.

What Does This Mean to Me?

Unbelief or a lack of faith in God's Word is the root of all forms of sin. Remember Romans 14:23, "…everything that does not come from faith is sin." All exterior, physical actions come from the inner condition. So, outward sins and outward good works are physical things that are dependent upon the inner spiritual condition of a person. If we had a choice of which part of our life to clean up first then, it is obvious that we should choose the inner one first as the outer flows from the inner.

Concentrate on fixing your inner life first. I once met a girl who said she quit smoking nine times. She told me, *"I am sure I will get it right one of these days if I keep on trying!"* But see, she is not removing the root. It is like trying to cure that sickness of ours by treating the symptoms and not the bacteria inside. There is a cure for the bacteria if you are willing to take the medicine! Cure the inner man first and the symptoms of the disease will leave. Clean the inside of the cup and the outside will be clean also.

How can you truly stop a sin if your inner being still yearns after it? If all you can think about is gambling, yet you do not gamble, are you free from sin? If all you can think about is alcohol, yet you do not drink, are you free from sin? First remove that inner desire and you will be clean. Cure the inner man first and the symptoms of the disease will leave.

Two

THE INDWELLING

efore you read this let me first make some preliminary comments. I know that many people like to make authoritative sounding statements, attach a few scriptures to them and then it becomes a doctrine. Later, others read it without proving it through the scripture and being led of the Spirit of God. Now that is exactly wrong and that is how people become misled. I realize that the things that I say or write will be held against me on the Day of Judgment, and I know if I *don't* say or write them it will be held against me on the Day of Judgment. We cannot bury the coin that is given us by God. So I am trying to be as honest, truthful, and sincere as I can because I do not want some people to be misled and think they are saved when they really are not.

No doubt there'll be many who disagree with this writing, but I want to prove it by the scriptures of the Bible. If you disagree then please first read the whole essay, take the scriptures, study them and pray and see if the Lord doesn't prove it to be right —ask the Lord to reveal it to you. All doctrine must be supported by the Word in every-way and in every angle. If you find me in error, then it is your responsibility to correct me using the Word.

For the purpose of this essay, I will be using the terms *indwelling* and *baptism* interchangeably as they are the same exact experience with the Holy Spirit.[3]

There are several questions that I wish to address in this writing. What is necessary for salvation? How do we know *when* we have eternal life? What is the *importance* of the baptism/indwelling of the Holy Ghost? What is the *purpose* of the baptism of the Holy Ghost? How do we know *when* we have the indwelling of the Holy Ghost? The answers to these questions are tied together. Also, I will try to weigh in on a long-standing debate, namely – can a person lose their salvation?

I am attempting to show that:

1. The indwelling of the Holy Spirit is a vital step in the salvation process

2. Spiritual faith or revelation IS proof of receiving the indwelling of the Holy Spirit

3. A person cannot lose their salvation once they have received the indwelling of the Holy Spirit

---

[3] Another essay, *Being Filled*, explains this in detail. The indwelling and baptism of the Holy Spirit are the same thing and the terms can be used interchangeably. Meanwhile, being *filled* with the Holy Spirit is a different experience. In general, for the purpose of this essay, I will use the terms "indwelling" in place of "baptism" because many people use the term "baptism" to mean "being filled," and I do not wish to add to the confusion.

Where Are We?

The indwelling of the Holy Spirit is NOT the first step on the path of salvation, justification is.[4] I said in the introduction of this book that I assume some level of prior knowledge and that I am assuming the reader is already justified or at least believes in it. Therefore, before I go on to explain the indwelling, let us do a short review of justification to show exactly where we are and where we are going. I feel that a person should always know exactly where they are in their walk with the Lord. A person should always be able to stand up and say, "*I am justified...*" or " *I am justified, and sanctified...*" A person should always know exactly where they are and where they are headed.

This great walk with God is full of **processes** that led to **states of being**. That is to say, the process of justification leads to a state of being justified. The process of sanctification leads to a state of being sanctified. Sometimes a person must attain one state before going onto the next. Other times not. For example, a person must be justified before they can go on with God and receive the indwelling, which is another, different state. On the other hand, the process of sanctification goes on throughout a person's life, perhaps until death, regardless if the person has received the indwelling.

So, we are going to review this process of justification, then move on to the significant step of the indwelling as one leads into the other. Roman 8:30 speaks about several of these different steps:

> Moreover whom He [God] did
> predestinate, them He also called:
> and whom He called, them He also

---

[4] Some people use the term "born again" or "saved" instead of justified or justification.

justified:
> and whom He justified, them He also
> glorified.

So there are certainly different steps in this salvation process. Justification is the first step.

Justification

The first step in the path toward salvation is believing that Jesus died on the cross and rose from the dead as an atoning sacrifice for our sins. In the Old Testament, an animal was sacrificed on an altar to take the place of the sinner because the penalty of sin is death. God allowed people to sacrifice animals to satisfy that penalty. Jesus came in the form of a kinsman redeemer to redeem us through His death.[5] If we believe that His sacrifice is sufficient to cover our sins, then it will. So then to receive eternal life we "only believe."

As you will see, it is one thing to believe something mentally and quite another to believe spiritually. This first step is justification and to be truly justified we must believe spiritually, not mentally.

Although justification is an internal process that changes the inside of a person, it usually can be identified from the outside by a public declaration of faith. As God works on a person's heart and changes them internally, the person comes to a place where

---

[5] See Ruth 4 and Leviticus 25 for more insight into the kinsman redeemer. God Himself took on human flesh through the virgin birth so that He would be a kinsman to the human race and therefore His shed blood would save us. According to the Old Testament law, only a kinsman could redeem a person condemned by the law.

they "give their life to God." Many Christian churches have formalized this into a ceremony such as adult baptism or publicly "accepting Jesus as your Savior."

But remember, the ceremony or external act by itself does not justify anyone. What must occur is for a seed of faith to be born inside the individual, for the individual to be changed internally by God.[6]

In Hebrews 11:6 it is written, "**Without faith it is impossible to please God**" and we must have faith in the saving blood of Jesus. There is nothing that we can do to be saved, we **only have to believe**. But how do we know **when** we believe? How do we know **when** our faith is sufficient in God's eyes?

Two Kinds of Faith

There are two different kinds of believing, that we can talk about: a mental–psychological kind and a spiritual kind.[7] The mental kind is the more common and occurs when we choose to hold fast to something in our mind. The spiritual can only be given by the Holy Spirit. Now remember we are talking about believing things that we cannot verify with our five senses. If we can verify it with our five senses then it is not faith, but knowledge.

For example, a person can tell you that it is sunny outside. If you feel that that person is a reliable source, then you might say, "*I believe you.*" Now, if you were told that you would die if they were wrong, would you say, "*I believe them unto death*"? You

---

[6] 1st John 3:9

[7] I use the word "believing" instead of "belief" because your faith must be active at all times.

would probably have some shadow of a doubt and want to peek out the door for yourself. Likewise, a person can be preached to, or read the Word, and *say* that they believe something in the Bible because it sounds good and makes sense. It is reasonable because it is the same message that many of us have heard since we were small kids. But do you believe it *truly*? Or is there a shadow of a doubt? Do you have a mental faith only or do you also have spiritual faith? I tell you that you **cannot** have spiritual faith and thus *truly* believe unless by the Holy Spirit.[8] In 1st Corinthians 12:3, Paul writes:

> Therefore I tell you that no one who is speaking by the Spirit of God says, '*Jesus be cursed,*' and **no one can say, '*Jesus is Lord,*' except by the Holy Spirit.**

Of course, any person can *say,* "*Jesus is Lord,*" with their mouth. Maybe they even think that they believe it. Maybe they were convinced of it by reasoning. Maybe they were raised to believe by the upbringing that their parents gave them. Maybe it just seems logical to them. But the Bible says, "**NO ONE can say, '*Jesus is Lord,*' EXCEPT by the Holy Spirit!**"

A mental-psychological belief is not good enough. If a person does not have the Spirit of Christ, they CANNOT truly be born again, they CANNOT be saved.

You might think, "*I stood up at the altar in front of everyone and gave my heart to Jesus, so I know I'm saved.*" Or say, "*I was baptized over here at the river, so I know I'm going to heaven.*" Now that is good that you did that, but if you did not get the confirmation from God that your faith was true, then where do you stand? If you do not have that inner seed of spiritual faith that comes by the Holy Spirit, then inside, in your heart of hearts, you

---

[8] Believing mentally is sometimes called "mental assent" when it is not accompanied with a spiritual belief

CANNOT *truly* know that *"Jesus is Lord"* and therefore are NOT saved.

Believing Unto Salvation

Now before the Holy Spirit can come, a person must first believe mentally. The Holy Spirit is not going to fall on an unrepentant sinner and **force** him or her to accept Jesus as their savior. So first develop a mental belief, and then the Holy Spirit will come and give you the spiritual belief. Once you have that spiritual belief; once that small seed of faith is placed deep inside of you, then you are justified. You are now believing *unto* salvation. You are now believing *unto* eternal life.

Romans 10:9 states, **"That if you confess with your mouth, '*Jesus is Lord*,' and believe in your heart that God raised him from the dead, you will be saved."** The person who believes in this statement from Paul and performs this confession is taking God at his Word and believing that God *will* save him or her.

But notice, you must believe WITH YOUR HEART. This is the process of Justification. Once the Holy Spirit comes and makes a change inside of you and gives you a spiritual faith you can stand up and declare, *"I am justified!"* The faith that we are talking about must be a heart faith, not a mental faith. It must be a spiritual faith, not a mental faith. You must receive a seed of faith from the Holy Spirit. You must receive the Spirit of Christ.

When you are justified, you are believing in **a future state** of salvation. You are not in heaven yet. You do not have the kingdom of God in you. You are just starting out, this is the first step. But what a step!

The Future State

Now we must pick up and move forward. Too many people stop at this first step and do not move on and this is a great mistake because your salvation is not yet secure. Up to this point you can still **lose** your salvation. Once you receive the indwelling, you cannot lose your salvation anymore. Of course, there are a tremendous amount of other benefits associated with the indwelling, so I urge you to attain it.

Notice how Paul talks about this "future state" of salvation when a person is justified in Roman 5:9-10:

> Much more then, **being now justified** by his blood, we **shall be saved** from wrath through Him.
> For if, when we were enemies, we were reconciled to God by the death of His Son, much more, being reconciled, we **shall be saved** by His life.

See that? When we are justified we are believing that we *will be* saved. We do not yet have salvation as a possession. Roman 5:1-2 also emphasizes this point:

> Therefore **being justified** by faith, we have peace with God through our Lord Jesus Christ:
> By whom also we have access by faith into this grace wherein we stand, and **rejoice in *hope* of** the glory of God.

One of the men who was on a cross next to Jesus was saved and he did not receive the baptism of the Holy Spirit, the indwelling. He may or may not have received water baptism, and was probably not sanctified. Yet Jesus said, *"Verily I say unto thee,*

Today shalt thou be with me in paradise."[9] What did this man have? Justification only. He made a confession of faith. He was justified, so he was saved. He believed in the saving blood of Jesus Christ and that is all that you need to be saved.[10]

But herein lies the problem. You see, that guy died minutes later and therefore did not have an opportunity to backslide or to lose his faith. I see too many people that only go to this first step and think they got it. They answered an altar call once, so they think they are saved. But when God knocks on the door of their heart asking them to go on, to give up the world and cleave to Him, what do they do? They lock the door, put bars on it and remove the door knob. They do not want to give up their evil ways. They do not want to give up the world. They do not want to look like those "holy roller" people. They do not want to be identified with Christ. There are a hundred reasons why, but these people should question if they still got it and repent.

Romans 13:11 emphasizes the point that when we are justified, we are believing in a future state of salvation:

> And that, knowing the time, that now it is high time to awake out of sleep: for **now is our salvation nearer than when we believed.**

We are justified **"when we believe."** What Paul is saying here is that **"now is our salvation nearer"** than when we were first justified. He says this because attaining eternal life is a future state that you are only believing *will happen* when you are justified. You do not yet have it. Some time had gone by, so Paul said salvation was nearer. They did not have it yet.

---

[9] Luke 23:43

[10] Some have argued that this man may have been baptized with water baptism by John the Baptist or one of the apostles. See Matthew 3:5, Mark 1:5 or Luke 3:3

Now I know there are some of you out there who are saying, "*Sure, we do not have eternal life yet. We do not have it until we die. Then we go to heaven.*" Not so, good friend. Jesus said that you could have eternal life **right now**, today, inside of you. Jesus said that you could have the kingdom of God inside of you.

Eternal Life

To live eternal life, a person must have an eternal spirit. Therefore, in order to possess eternal life, we must possess the Eternal Spirit which is the Holy Spirit. In John 5:24, Jesus says:

> *I tell you the truth, whoever hears My word and believes Him who sent Me* **has eternal life** *and will not be condemned;* **he has crossed over from death to life.**

This word "*eternal life*" in this quote is the word " Zoë " in Greek - ζωην. Zoë, pronounced *dzo-ay'*, means "the life of God." We must have God's life in us. We must have God's Spirit in us. Let us substitute the meaning of the words and see how it reads:

> *I tell you the truth, whoever hears My word and believes Him who sent Me* **has the life of God [inside of them]** *and will not be condemned;* **he has crossed over from death to life.**

We must receive the indwelling of the Holy Spirit, then we HAVE eternal life. We have God's life in us. Before that, we only have faith that God *will* do the work. 1st Corinthians 6:17 says, **"But he who unites himself with the Lord is one with Him in spirit."**

When the Holy Spirit comes and a person receives the indwelling of the Spirit, they are baptized with the Spirit like on the day of Pentecost. The person is greatly changed.[11] After being converted they are no longer believing *unto* a future state of salvation but *have* salvation. They have the "kingdom of heaven" inside of them. **They have the "kingdom of God" inside of them.** They are not believing they *will be* saved, they ARE saved. They have eternal life as a possession. They own it. In Luke 17:20-21, it says:

> **And when He was demanded of the Pharisees, when the kingdom of God should come, He [Jesus] answered them and said,** *"The kingdom of God cometh not with observation:*
>
> *Neither shall they say, 'Lo here! or, lo there!' for, behold, **the kingdom of God is within you.**"*

When WE receive the indwelling of the Holy Spirit, WE become a part of the kingdom of heaven. In fact the kingdom of God is inside of us, because God is inside of us!

---

[11] So there are two changes. the first when we are justified, the second when we receive the indwelling.

Can a Person Lose Salvation?

Now once we have received the indwelling, God places a seal on us. A seal is a sign of a finished work. Any manufactured product has a seal on it so that you know that it has not been tampered with. In Ephesians 4:30, it is written:

> And grieve not the **Holy Spirit** of God, whereby **ye are sealed unto the day of redemption**.

By this we know that we cannot lose our salvation once we achieve this point. Before this we are believing *towards* salvation – that is we are believing that we are *going* to be saved up to this point. But once we reach this point, we ARE saved. We have received the indwelling of the Holy Spirit and we are sealed. When we received the indwelling of the Holy Spirit, we are sealed **until the day of our redemption**.

Once a person is sealed, they CANNOT lose salvation – they have it until the day of redemption. But before a person is sealed, they can still lose their salvation. Before a person is sealed, they only believe that they *will* be saved at some future time. Until you received the indwelling, you can still backslide out, change your mind and disbelieve, and head straight to Hell. Once you received the indwelling of the Holy Spirit, it is finished – you are saved and have eternal security. In Ephesians 1:13-14, Paul writes:

> In whom ye also trusted, after that ye heard the word of truth, the gospel of your salvation:
>
> in whom also **after that ye believed, ye were sealed with that Holy Spirit of promise**,
>
> which is the **earnest** of our inheritance until the redemption of the purchased possession, unto the praise of his glory.

When the Holy Spirit comes, you will be sealed with the "earnest." The Holy Spirit is the earnest. This word "**earnest**" is sometimes translated "guarantee" or "down payment" and in Greek is the word αρραβων. This word can also be translated as "engagement ring." 2nd Corinthians 5:5 says:

Now He that hath prepared us for the selfsame thing is God, who **also hath given unto us the Spirit as a guarantee.**

When you hear the Word, there should be something stirring deep inside you –maybe a "still quiet voice" that you *need* to respond to. Be led by the Spirit. Don't think you are done just because you answered an altar call once, ten years ago. Yes, you may have "called on the name of the Lord" and asked to be saved. But did you listen to the Spirit when he answered your call? Did you do what He led you to do? Take the next step and be baptized by the Holy Ghost and have salvation as a possession.

The Holy Spirit communicates with people but they do not want to answer. God calls. God calls sinners who are still up to their necks in sin. God talks to everyone. When you start your walk in faith, God talks to you. As you grow closer and closer, God talks to you. God never stops this. God loves his children and He loves to communicate with them. All you have to do is open up to Him. In Revelation 3:20, God says:

Behold, I stand at the door, and knock: if any man hear My voice, and open the door, I will come in to him, and will sup with him, and he with Me.

The Change

The change that takes place when a person receives the indwelling is significant. A person cannot even accept things of God before having God's Spirit inside of them. In 1st Corinthians 2:14 Paul writes:

The man without the Spirit does not *accept* the things that come from the Spirit of God, for they are foolishness to him, and he cannot understand them, because they are spiritually discerned.

When you are justified, there is a change that takes place deep inside of you, but it is not the only change. When you receive the indwelling, your nature is changed, the blinders come off, you can see things the way God wants you to see them. When you receive the indwelling, you see the world for what it truly is.

Baptism

In Mark 16:15-16, Jesus says:
Go into all the world and preach the good news to all creation.

*Whoever believes **and is baptized** will be saved, but whoever does not believe will be condemned.*

Many people mistakenly believe that the baptism Jesus speaks of is water baptism. This is an error. We need a Holy Spirit baptism to be sealed away forever in the kingdom of God.

In Matthew 3:11, John the Baptist says:
> *I baptize you with water for repentance.*
> *But after me will come one who is more*
> *powerful than I, whose sandals I am not fit*
> *to carry.* **He will baptize you with the**
> **Holy Spirit** *and with fire.*

Clearly, the baptism that Jesus came to bring was not water baptism but spiritual baptism with the Holy Spirit. In John 3:5, Jesus answered Nicodemus:

> *I tell you the truth, **no one can enter***
> ***the kingdom of God unless he is***
> ***born of water AND the Spirit.***

When you receive the Holy Ghost baptism, you "enter the kingdom of God." God comes to live inside of you as a person. You enter the kingdom of God and the kingdom of God is inside of you. The two become one. This does not happen in water baptism.

When the Holy Spirit comes and a person receives the indwelling of the Spirit, they are baptized with the Spirit like on the day of Pentecost. The person is changed. After being converted they are no longer believing *unto* a future state of salvation but *have* salvation.

Father, Son, and Holy Ghost

My next point requires an understanding of the offices of God as Father, Son, and Holy Spirit. There are different offices of God and each different office is involved in different phases of the salvation process. There is only one God, but God presents Himself differently in different areas. Therefore, I am going to explain the different offices or titles of God first before I make this next point.

Let me explain the offices of God using myself as an example. I am a man who has children and is married. Of course, I also have parents. So, first let me describe my *offices*. I am a father, I am a son, I am a husband, I am an electrician, and of course there are other things that I am. Now in each of these *offices*, there is a different relationship with the people associated with that *office*. So, I have a certain way of acting when I am with my parents that I might not display to my wife. Likewise, I act differently toward my supervisor than my children. So, although I am the same person, I might act differently to different people depending upon my relationship with that person. But I am still the same one person.

Additionally, the people in these relationships have different levels of access to me depending upon the relationship. For example, my children can ask me for things that my wife or my parents could not. Now this is similar to the offices of God as Father, Son, and Holy Spirit. God is one God, but has three offices. We have a certain access to God as the Father. We have a certain access to God as the Son and a certain access to God as the Holy Spirit. They all have different jobs and relationships with us and yet they all three are all the same one God only in different *offices*.

So, what I have just done is given a simplistic explanation of God as Father, Son, and Holy Ghost.[12] With that understanding, let us read Roman 8:5-11:

> **For they that are after the flesh do mind**
> **the things of the flesh;**
> **but they that are after the Spirit the things**

---

[12] There is a much deeper revelation of the Godhead. I am only giving this simple explanation in order to prove my point.

of the Spirit.

For to be carnally minded *is* death;
but to be spiritually minded *is* life and peace.

Because the carnal mind *is* enmity against God: for it is not subject to the law of God, neither indeed can be.

So then they that are in the flesh cannot please God.

But ye are not in the flesh, but in the Spirit, if so be that the **Spirit of God dwell** in you.

Now if any man have not the **Spirit of Christ**, he is none of His.

And if **Christ *be* in you**, the **body *is* dead** because of sin;

but the Spirit *is* life because of **righteousness**.

But if the **Spirit** of him that raised up Jesus from the dead *dwell* **in you**, He that raised up Christ from the dead shall also **quicken your mortal bodies by His Spirit that *dwelleth* in you**.

This is one of the most powerful passages that displays the difference between being justified and having the indwelling.

First, know that the office of Christ is the office that deals with justification. This is because we are accepting Christ as our Savior. We are welcoming Jesus into our hearts. So, what does this passage say about the work of the Spirit of Christ:

Now if any man have not the Spirit of Christ, he is none of His.

And if Christ *be* in you, the body *is* dead because of sin; but the Spirit *is* life because of righteousness.

This first line says that if you do not have the Spirit of Christ, you are still condemned. Clearly, receiving the Spirit of Christ is the first step. It is justification. It is being born again.

When we become justified, we are accepting the gift of righteousness that Jesus gives. We are being made just, or righteous. We are judged as being on the right side of the law. But we can always lose that. We have Christ in us in the form of a little seed of faith in the saving blood of Jesus.

In the second line, we see that we are changed in a fashion but we still have to deal with a body that is spiritually dead. It says:

> And if Christ *be* in you, the body *is* dead because of sin; but the Spirit *is* life because of righteousness.

We are still full of a body of death. We have a tiny seed of faith in us surrounded by dead, carnal flesh that still yearns after the things of the world. It says when you have "**Christ in you**" that your "**body *is* dead.**" Your body is still fleshly, worldly, carnal, and spiritually dead.

But what is the difference when we receive the indwelling? It is a work of the Father. Remember, it is the same God, only a different work, a different office, a different level of access, and a different manifestation of the Spirit. When we are indwelt, we receive the Spirit of God the Father INSIDE of us:

> But ye are not in the flesh, but in the Spirit, if so be that **the Spirit of God *dwell* in you**...
> But **if the Spirit [of God]...** *dwell* **in you**, He... shall **also quicken your mortal bodies by His Spirit that *dwelleth* in you**.

See that? Here Paul is giving a clue as to one of the great

things that will happen with the indwelling. First, we are no longer IN the flesh. When we only had justification we were still stuck with this dead, carnal, fleshly body. Now, we are " **not in the flesh, but in the Spirit.**" We see that our mortal bodies will be "quickened." To quicken is to make alive spiritually. So, what this means is that our five natural senses will be heightened to spiritual things. We will have something like a six sense. [13]

When we are justified, we have the Spirit of Christ in us, but our body is still spiritually dead. We have a seed of the Spirit of Christ surrounded by a dead, fleshly body. When we receive the indwelling of the Holy Spirit, we have the Spirit of God placed inside of us and our bodies are quickened. Now, the whole unit is made spiritually alive!

Entering the Kingdom

Another scripture that displays the difference between the work of the Spirit of Christ (justification)and the work of the Spirit of God (the indwelling) is John 3:3-5. And remember, it is the same one God only in different offices. Here Jesus is explaining to Nicodemus about being born again:

Jesus answered and said unto him, *"Verily, verily, I say unto thee, **Except a man be born again, he cannot SEE the kingdom of God. ***"*
Nicodemus saith unto Him, *"How can a man be born when he is old? Can he enter the second time into his mother's womb, and be born?"*

---

[13] This is not the only thing that happens with the indwelling. I list several more in the chapter called *Being Filled*, but there are many others.

> Jesus answered, *"Verily, verily, I say unto thee,* **Except a man be born of water and of the Spirit, he cannot ENTER into the kingdom of God."**

The first experience, being born again, being justified, allows a person to SEE the kingdom. It opens your awareness to spiritual things. Before a person is born again, they cannot see anything spiritual. Once we become justified, we are reborn. We do not enter the kingdom yet, we are not yet sealed, but we can SEE what is going on somewhat. It is a start.

2nd Corinthians 5:17 tells us that the new birth is a work of the Spirit of Christ. This is something that happens in justification:

> Therefore if any man **be in Christ**, let him be a **new creature**: old things are passed away; behold, all things are become new.

Next, we go on with God and receive the indwelling of the Holy Spirit:

> Jesus answered, *"Verily, verily, I say unto thee,* **Except a man be born of water and of the Spirit, he cannot ENTER into the kingdom of God."**

Now we are *"born of water and of the Spirit,"* and we ENTER the kingdom of God. We are sealed. The Holy Spirit comes to indwell. We enter the kingdom of God because the kingdom of God is inside of us.

When a person is born of the Spirit, they enter the kingdom of God. We are born of the Spirit when we receive the baptism of the Holy Spirit. Then we enter the kingdom of God because the Holy Spirit, the eternal Spirit of God takes up permanent residence

42

inside of us. Then the kingdom of God is inside of us. In Luke 17:20-21, it says:

> And when He was demanded of the Pharisees, when the kingdom of God should come, He [Jesus] answered them and said, *"The kingdom of God cometh not with observation:*
>
> *Neither shall they say, 'Lo here! or, lo there!' for, behold, the kingdom of God is within you."*

When we receive the Holy Spirit, we receive God's Spirit. God's Spirit is Zoë, which is eternal life. God's Spirit is light and life. When we have Zoë inside of us, we have eternal life in the form of God's Spirit residing inside of us. Eternal life can live inside of us! We have eternal life if we have God's Spirit living inside. 1st John 3:15 says:

> Whosoever hates his brother is a murderer: and ye know that no murderer hath eternal life abiding in him.

We could just as easily rewrite this to say:

> ...ye know that no murderer hath the the Spirit of God abiding in him.

In Mark 9:1 Jesus tells the Apostles that some of them will not die until they see the kingdom of God. How is this possible? It is because the kingdom of God came at Pentecost! The kingdom of God comes with the baptism of Holy Spirit!

> And He [Jesus] said unto them, *"Verily I say unto you, That there be some of them that stand here,* **which shall not taste of death, till they have seen the kingdom of God come** *with power."*

We enter the kingdom of God when we receive the baptism of the Holy Spirit. It is a spiritual happening. This is not something that can occur through much studying in Bible College or any physical work. It can only come through the Holy Spirit. Paul says this in 1st Corinthians:

> For **the kingdom of God is not in word**, but in power. (4:20)

> Now this I say, brethren, that **flesh and blood cannot inherit the kingdom of God**; neither doth corruption inherit incorruption. (15:50)

The kingdom of God is only obtained through the Holy Spirit. Your physical condition does not matter! Seek the Holy Spirit! Too many people try to clean up their lives first. You can never fully clean up your life without the Holy Spirit anyway. Seek the Holy Spirit first with every effort and every ounce of your being. Romans 14:17 says:

> For **the kingdom of God is not meat and drink**; but righteousness, and peace, and joy in the Holy Ghost.

It does not matter what you are eating or drinking. It does not matter if you still smoke and swear. Seek the kingdom of God FIRST. In Luke 12:29-31, Jesus says:

> *And seek not ye what ye shall eat, or what ye shall drink, neither be ye of doubtful mind.*
>
> *For all these things do the nations of the world seek after: and your Father knoweth that ye have need of these things.*
>
> *But rather seek ye the kingdom of God; and all these things shall be added unto you.*

And in Matthew 6:33, Jesus says:

> **But seek ye FIRST the kingdom of God**, *and His righteousness; and all these things shall be added unto you.*

Seek the kingdom of God FIRST. Seek the baptism of the Holy Spirit FIRST. Then once you have the Holy Spirit, the Holy Spirit will teach you all things.

There are two different changes that take place. Being born again (justified) is the first birth. Being born of the Spirit (receiving the indwelling) is the second change that takes place. There are two distinct changes that take place and different things that happen with each. Do not stop after the first. Seek the Holy Spirit.

Peter

The first step is justification, which is believing that God will save the person. Next comes the Baptism of the Holy Ghost. For an example of these two different steps, let us look at Peter. First the disciples are justified – they are chosen by Jesus to be his followers, and they choose to follow Him. This is the act of faith. In modern times this act of faith is making a public declaration that you are a Christian: standing at the altar and giving your life to Jesus or water baptism are examples of a public declaration of faith.

After some space of time, the apostles go out into the world performing miracles. Jesus gave them power to heal the sick, cast out devils, raise the dead, and they come back rejoicing.[14] **Yet they were still not converted and they could still lose their faith.** They could still slip into unbelief and head straight to Hell. Look at Luke 22:31-34 where Jesus addresses Simon Peter:

> And the Lord said, *"Simon, Simon, behold, Satan hath desired to have you, that he may sift you as wheat: But I have prayed for thee, that **thy faith fail not**: and **when thou art converted,** strengthen thy brethren."*
>
> And he [Simon] said unto him, *"Lord, I am ready to go with thee, both into prison, and to death."*
>
> And He [Jesus] said, *"I tell thee, Peter, the cock shall not crow this day, before that thou shalt thrice deny that thou knowest Me."*

Notice that Jesus says Peter's faith *could* fail, there is still a possibility of backsliding and disbelieving at this point. He could still slip back into unbelief. Peter was only justified.

Also, Peter did not go through the full conversion yet. Notice how Jesus said, **"when thou art converted."** So, at this point Peter's nature is still not changed. He did not have the kingdom of God in him. He did not have the indwelling in him. We already know that Peter denies even knowing Jesus later that night.

After Jesus dies on the cross and returns to earth to visit with the apostles the following discourse takes place, as written in John 21:15-18:

---

[14] See Luke 9:1-6 or Matthew 10:5-6

> When they had finished eating, Jesus said to Simon Peter, *"Simon son of John, do you **truly** love Me more than these?"*
>
> "Yes, Lord," he said, "*You know that I love You.*"
>
> Jesus said, *"Feed My lambs."*
>
> Again Jesus said, *"Simon son of John, do You **truly** love Me?"*
>
> He answered, "*Yes, Lord, you know that I love You.*"
>
> Jesus said, *"Take care of My sheep."*
>
> The third time He said to him, *"Simon son of John, do you love Me?"*
>
> Peter was hurt because Jesus asked him the third time, *"Do you love Me?"*
>
> He said, "*Lord, you know all things; You know that I love You.*"
>
> Jesus said, *"Feed My sheep.."*

Jesus is pointing out a *lack* of godly love in Peter. Peter is looking at the common love he knows and thinks, *"I got it, yes, I love You."* Jesus is looking at that Holy Spirit filled love and pointing out that, *"No, you don't got it, you don't **truly** love Me – you can't, you don't have the Holy Ghost yet."* **You cannot have godly love without God inside of you.**

Now we know that Peter was even afraid to acknowledge that he knew the Lord Jesus before, denying Him three times while Jesus was being questioned, but look what happens when Peter gets the Holy Spirit in Acts chapter 2:

> When the day of Pentecost came, they were all together in one place.
>
> **Suddenly a sound like a rushing mighty wind came from heaven and filled the whole house where they were sitting.**

They saw what seemed to be tongues of fire that separated and came to rest on each of them.

All of them were filled with the Holy Spirit and began to speak in other tongues as the Spirit enabled them.

Now there were staying in Jerusalem God-fearing Jews from every nation under heaven.

When they heard this sound, a crowd came together in bewilderment, because each one heard them speaking in his own language.

Utterly amazed, they asked: "*Are not all these men who are speaking Galileans?*

Then how is it that each of us hears them in his own native language?

Parthians, Medes and Elamites; residents of Mesopotamia, Judea and Cappadocia, Pontus and Asia, Phrygia and Pamphylia, Egypt and the parts of Libya near Cyrene; visitors from Rome, both Jews and converts to Judaism, Cretans and Arabs—we hear them declaring the wonders of God in our own tongues!"

Amazed and perplexed, they asked one another, "*What does this mean?*"

Some, however, made fun of them and said, "*They have had too much wine.*"

Then **Peter stood up** with the Eleven, **raised his voice** and addressed the crowd: "*Fellow Jews and all of you who live in Jerusalem, let me explain this to you; listen carefully to what I say.*

These men are not drunk, as you suppose. It's only nine in the morning!

No, this is what was spoken by the prophet Joel:

'In the last days, God says, "I will
pour out my Spirit on all people.

Your sons and daughters will prophesy,
your young men will see visions, your old men
will dream dreams.

Even on my servants, both men and women, I
will pour out my Spirit in those days, and
they will prophesy.

I will show wonders in the heaven
above and signs on the earth below, blood and
fire and billows of smoke.

The sun will be turned to darkness and
the moon to blood before the coming of the
great and glorious day of the Lord.

And everyone who calls on the name of
the Lord will be saved.'"

So, if we could put it in order, Peter is not saved, just a fisherman whom Jesus calls out to follow Him. Peter chooses to follows Jesus because he mentally believes Jesus. At some point Peter receives a spiritual belief and a small seed of faith is placed in his heart. He is saved in that he is justified, but he could still lose his salvation. He could still slip back into unbelief at this point. Remember jesus said that Peter's faith COULD fail. He is not yet sealed.

Peter casts out demons in Jesus name along with Judas and the others,[15] and then Peter, cowardly, denies even knowing Jesus. Still the same. After Jesus leaves them the second time, Peter and the others are hiding, cowardly, in an upper room in Jerusalem so that the priests won't find them. Their nature is still not changed yet. They have a seed of faith surrounded by the shell of a carnal man.

---

[15] Luke 9:1-6. Matthew 10:5-6

Then the Holy Spirit comes and they receive It.[16] Now they are sealed away forever as sons of God. They all roll out of the room with boldness –preaching the gospel, which is good works, because the Spirit leads them to. They have no more fear of the high priests; they have faith and love of God in them because they are filled and indwelled with the Holy Spirit.

Do not rely on a mental-psychological belief that "*I love God and that's good enough,*" like Peter did initially. Meet Jesus and have an experience. Get the Holy Spirit. Let the Spirit lead you and change you. Not just in order to go to heaven when you die while you continue to live your same old life down here on earth. There is a prize to be had here on earth: the Spirit will change your nature. Remember, in Galatians 5:22-25, Paul writes:

> But the fruit of the Spirit is love, joy, peace, patience, kindness, goodness, faithfulness, gentleness and self-control.
> Against such things there is no law.
> Those who belong to Christ Jesus have crucified the sinful nature with its passions and desires.
> Since we live by the Spirit, let us keep in step with the Spirit.

You won't be depressed or unhappy anymore, and when hardship comes, it won't bother you like it used to. And yes, you will do good works. But not because "it is expected of a good Christian," you will actually *want* to do them and *enjoy* doing them.

---

[16] I believe several of the apostles received the indwelling earlier, when Jesus breathed on them in John 20:22. But, not all of them were present at both times. Notice that at Pentecost the Holy Spirit appeared in both wind and fire, as both indwelling and filling. More on this in the essay *Being Filled.*

Evidence of the Holy Ghost

So far we have seen that to truly have eternal life, to have salvation as a possession, we must have the indwelling of the Holy Ghost. So, how do we know *when* we have it? What is *the evidence* of the indwelling of the Holy Spirit?

First, I would like to go through a few ideas that have been put up by others, and then I will show you the truth, if you can accept it. Some of these are long standing doctrines of some of the larger denominations. I have no intention of bashing another person's belief or doctrine, but like I said in the beginning, I only want people to be sure that they are saved. If we are holding fast to a doctrine and basing our salvation on that doctrine, then we have to make sure that the doctrine is correct.[17]

Evidence of the Holy Ghost: The Process?

One doctrine is that a person receives the baptism of the Holy Ghost due to a set of steps or a process such as the sacrament of Confirmation. This sacrament is held during the process of the Mass and the people who are to receive are lined up at the front of the church and the priest either shakes your hand or puts his hand on your shoulder and says some words. I went through this when I was thirteen and this is how I remember it. Now this may or may not be a process that works, but if there is no sign or evidence following the process, we cannot even discuss it to answer our question. We want to know what the evidence is.

---

[17] Also, I might add that many denominations have varying beliefs and I am just covering these very briefly and only covering the main idea without any shades of variation.

Now, I have seen people receive the Holy Spirit using a process or a set of steps, but we cannot say that everyone who does a set of steps will definitely receive. The set of steps is not a guarantee. It is not evidence. Receiving the Holy Spirit is not determinant upon a process.

Evidence of the Holy Ghost: When We Believe?

Another doctrine is that a person receives the Holy Ghost *at the same time* that they believe. That is, when the confession of faith is made the Holy Spirit enters in and starts His work of sanctification. Obviously people can make a false confession which is just words, but if a person makes a true confession then they are saved according to this doctrine. But in Acts 19:1-2, Luke writes:

> While Apollos was at Corinth, Paul took the road through the interior and arrived at Ephesus.
> He said unto them, '*Have ye received the Holy Ghost **since** ye **believed**?*'
> And they said unto him, '*We have not so much as heard whether there be any Holy Ghost.*'

Luke clearly makes a distinction between believing and receiving the Holy Spirit. They are two separate events. Therefore, this doctrine of receiving the Holy Ghost *when we believe* does not agree with the Word.

Now, if I can make a subtle point. When we become justified, we receive a seed of faith and the Spirit of Christ does this work. The Holy Spirit does start to work on you, so in that sense, you *do* receive the Holy Spirit. But this is in no way the same as receiving the indwelling of the Holy Spirit. Receiving the indwelling is when the Spirit of God comes to dwell inside of you.

Receiving the indwelling is when the Spirit of God takes up permanent residence inside of you and never leaves.[18]

Evidence of the Holy Ghost: Speaking in Tongues?

Yet another doctrine is that the evidence of the Holy Spirit is speaking in tongues. What the scriptures reveal is that speaking in tongues *can be* a manifestation of the Holy Spirit but it is not *proof* that a person has the Holy Spirit. In 1st Corinthians 12:4-11, Paul writes:

> Now there are **diversities of gifts, but the same Spirit**.
> And there are differences of administrations, but the same Lord.
> And there are diversities of operations, but it is the same God which worketh all in all.
> But the manifestation of the Spirit is given to every man to profit withal.
> For to one is given by the Spirit the word of wisdom; to another the word of knowledge by the same Spirit; to another faith by the same Spirit; to another the gifts of healing by the same Spirit; to another the working of miracles; to another prophecy; to another discerning of spirits; to another divers kinds of tongues; to another the interpretation of tongues: **but all these worketh that one and the selfsame Spirit, dividing to every man severally as He will.**

_____

[18] Another subtle point. Although the Holy Spirit never leaves when you have the indwelling, there will be times when you will not be able to detect His presence with your five senses.

So, we see that all of these manifestations are from the same Holy Spirit. Do not limit God to only one of these manifestations. In Acts 19:6-7, Paul starts off by saying:

> "John's baptism was a baptism of repentance.
> He told the people to believe in the one coming after him, that is, in Jesus."
> On hearing this, they were baptized into the name of the Lord Jesus.
> When Paul placed his hands on them, the Holy Spirit came on them, and they spoke in tongues **and prophesied**.
> There were about twelve men in all.

In this case the people receiving the Holy Ghost showed two different manifestations of the Spirit, tongues AND prophesy. Therefore, to say that the evidence of the Holy Spirit is speaking in tongues ONLY does not agree with the Word. First, a person receives the Holy Spirit, then that person may have a manifestation of the Spirit. It may or may not be tongues.

Notice that we have no record of Jesus speaking in tongues until he was on the cross,[19] yet he displayed all the other manifestations of the Spirit in the three years previous to the cross.[20] Do we say that Jesus did not have the Holy Spirit until He was hanging on the cross? What about John the Baptist? The Bible says he received the Holy Spirit in his mother's womb.[21] Did he speak in tongues inside there?

---

[19] Matthew 27:46 says: And about the ninth hour Jesus cried with a loud voice, saying, *"Eli, Eli, lama sabachthani?"*

[20] Some have argued that Jesus' ministry was three and a half years.

[21] See Luke 1:41.

Another point against this doctrine is that tongues can be a gift. Yet, Romans 11:29 says, "Gifts and callings are without repentance." So, we do not need to repent to receive a gift, such as speaking in tongues. But, how can a person have eternal life without repenting? The above doctrine says that the evidence of receiving the Holy Spirit and therefore the evidence of having God inside of them is speaking in tongues. But right here in *Romans*, it says that a person can receive the gift without repenting.

Probably my biggest point against this doctrine is that the Devil can imitate spiritual gifts. If we say that anyone who speaks in tongues has the Holy Ghost and then we see a witch doctor under the influence of the Devil speak in tongues, where are we then? Any physical manifestation can be imitated by the evil one, so they cannot be an *absolute* proof of having the indwelling of the Holy Spirit.

Evidence of the Holy Ghost: Feeling?

Another one I have heard is that people say that they can *feel* the presence of the Holy Spirit. They say that they know they have the Holy Spirit because they *feel* that goose-bumpy, tingling, anointing sensation when the Holy Spirit falls on them.

John Wesley was probably the most famous person to describe this. He said that when he was converted on May 24, 1738, his *"heart was strangely warmed."* He said he had a conversion, a deep and unmistakable experience of faith associated with this warming sensation.

Now, I have felt that too. I have felt the goose bumps, the fire, the rivers of flowing water[22], the anointing sensation, all of it. But understand that ANYTHING felt physically can be imitated by the Devil and therefore cannot be used to *prove* that a person has the Holy Spirit.

Evidence of the Holy Ghost: Fruit of the Spirit?

Yet another doctrine is that the evidence of the Holy Spirit is having the *fruit of the Spirit*. First, In Matthew 7:17-20 Jesus says:

> *Even so, every good tree brings forth good fruit; but a corrupt tree brings forth evil fruit.*
> *A good tree cannot bring forth evil fruit, neither can a corrupt tree bring forth good fruit.*
> *Every tree that brings not forth good fruit is hewn down, and cast into the fire.*
> *Wherefore by their fruits ye shall know them.*

Next, it is written in Galatians 5:22-25,

> **But the fruit of the Spirit is love, joy, peace, long-suffering, gentleness, goodness, faith, meekness, temperance**: against such there is no law.
> And they that are Christ's have crucified the flesh with the affections and lusts.

---

[22] John 7:38

56

> If we live in the Spirit, let us also walk in
> the Spirit.

With these two scriptures put together, the conclusion is drawn that the evidence of having the Holy Spirit is the fruits of the person's life. If the person is full of love, joy, peace, long-suffering, gentleness, goodness, faith, meekness, and temperance, they **must be** indwelt with the Holy Spirit according to this doctrine.

Unfortunately, we can find many counter-examples of people who have all of these characteristics and are not Christians. In fact, not to be irreverent, but Jesus tore up the temple moneychangers and that was not inline with this list of characteristics.

Now, I do agree that a person who has the indwelling of the Holy Spirit will be full of godly love and the other characteristics on this list. But this proof does not work in reverse, not everyone full of love has the indwelling. Additionally, the Devil can imitate any emotion just as much as he can imitate spiritual gifts.

comments

Now I will tell you what is the true evidence of a person having the Holy Spirit, but first a few comments. The above proofs all have some elements of truth in them. Certainly, someone who is indwelt with the Holy Spirit will show manifestations of spiritual gifts such as speaking in tongues. Likewise, someone who is indwelt with the Holy Spirit will generally have the fruits of love, joy, peace, long-suffering, gentleness, goodness, faith, meekness, and temperance among others. Also, most all people experience that goose-bumpy, tingling, anointing sensation when the Holy Spirit falls on them. But my point is not that you will not have these physical manifestations, but that they do not *prove* you have the Holy Ghost. When you receive the Holy Spirit, there will be a manifestation. Something spiritual will happen. You might not be able to see it on the outside, but something WILL happen. But what I am saying is that you can have these manifestations and *not* have the indwelling.

The indwelling comes first, then the signs *follow*. But it does not work in reverse. Just because you have the sign, does not mean you have the indwelling. Let me repeat that. When the Holy Spirit comes on you, there *will* be some external things happen. Some shout, others feel strong conviction and cry, others speak in tongues, and other dance in the spirit. I am not saying that these things do not happen. They do happen. What I am saying is that they do not prove anything. They can all be imitated by the Devil. Now, let us see what the Word says about the evidence of the Holy Spirit.

Revelation Is the Evidence of the Indwelling of the Holy Spirit

We have already seen that the Devil can imitate any outward physical manifestation whether it is a spiritual gift like speaking in tongues or an emotion like love or a goose-bumpy, tingling, sensation. Any sensation that a person can feel with their five senses can be imitated by evil spirits. So the proof of the indwelling cannot be external, it must be something internal. It must be something spiritual. It must be something that the Devil cannot imitate.

The evidence of the indwelling of the Holy Ghost comes by **spiritual revelation**. The Holy Spirit must tell you, not in your mind, but deep down in your heart, deep down in your spirit, that you are indwelt. This knowledge is spiritual and can come only by the Holy Spirit. It is not a mental-faith knowledge that is gained through intellectual understanding. It is a spiritual revelation that occurs when the Holy Spirit speaks to a person's spirit. John 14:26 says:

> *But the Comforter, which is the Holy Ghost, whom the Father will send in my name,* ***He shall teach you ALL things, and bring all things to your remembrance,*** *whatsoever I have said unto you.*

Also, it is written in 1st Corinthians 2:9-10:

> But as it is written, **Eye hath not seen, nor ear heard, neither have entered into the heart of man**, the things which God hath prepared for them that love him.
>
> **But God hath *revealed* them unto us by his Spirit**: for the Spirit searcheth all things, yea, the deep things of God.
>
> For who among men knows the thoughts of a man except the man's spirit within him? In the same way no one knows the thoughts of God except the Spirit of God.

So we cannot see it physically because **"Eye hath not seen"** and we cannot hear it physically because **"nor ear heard"** and we cannot know anything by emotion because **"neither have entered into the heart of man"**. But how are all spiritual things *truly* known? By spiritual revelation because **"God hath *revealed* them unto us by his Spirit."**

Jesus tells us clearly that the church is built upon spiritual revelation. And remember that the word *church* means "the called out ones." God's true *church* is his people, not a building. In Matthew 16:13-18, it is written:

When Jesus came into the coasts of Caesarea Philippi, He asked His disciples, saying, *"Whom do men say that I the Son of man am?"*

And they said, *"Some say that Thou art John the Baptist: some, Elias; and others, Jeremias, or one of the prophets."*

He saith unto them, *"But whom say ye that I am?"*

And Simon Peter answered and said, *"Thou art the Christ, the Son of the living God."*

And Jesus answered and said unto him, *"Blessed art thou, Simon Barjona: for flesh and blood hath not **revealed** it unto thee, but My Father which is in heaven.*

*And I say also unto thee, that thou art Peter, **and upon this rock I will build my church;** and the gates of hell shall not prevail against it."*[23]

The fact that the apostle's names were written in heaven was known by revelation to them. In Luke 10:20-22, Jesus says:

*"Notwithstanding in this rejoice not, that the spirits are subject unto you; but rather **rejoice, because your names are written in heaven."***

---

[23] For a more detailed analysis of this scripture, see the *On This Rock* essay.

In that hour Jesus rejoiced in spirit, and said, *"I thank thee, O Father, Lord of heaven and earth, that Thou hast hid these things from the wise and prudent, and* **hast revealed them unto babes:** *even so, Father; for so it seemed good in Thy sight.*

All things are delivered to Me of My Father: and no man knoweth who the Son is, but the Father; and who the Father is, but the Son, and he to **whom the Son will reveal** *him."*

Finally, Romans 8:16 says:
The Spirit Itself beareth witness with our spirit, that we are the children of God.

Importance and Purpose of the Holy Ghost

Now, we know that we must have the Holy Ghost, and we know how to know when we got It. So, what should we expect the Holy Ghost to lead us to do?

The purpose of the Holy Spirit is to continue the works that Jesus started. In John 14:12, Jesus says:
Verily, verily, I say unto you, He that believeth on Me, **the works that I do shall he do also;** *and greater works than these shall he do; because I go unto my Father.*

The work that we are to continue is spreading the gospel. Now before you jump to the conclusion that "spreading the gospel" means preaching only, let us see what the Bible says.

Spreading the gospel is NOT to be done with words only, but as Paul says, in power and demonstration of the Holy Ghost. In 1st Corinthians 1:17, Paul writes:

> For Christ sent me not to baptize, but to preach the gospel: **not with wisdom of words**, lest the cross of Christ should be made of none effect.

Then in 1st Corinthians 2:4-5, he continues:

> And my speech and my preaching was not with enticing words of man's wisdom, **but in demonstration of the Spirit and of power:** that your faith should not stand in the wisdom of men, but in the power of God.

The signs or manifestations of the Holy Spirit are very important and are to *follow* the preached Word as a vindication that the gospel message is true. Jesus said in John 10:37-38:

> *If I do not the works of My Father, believe Me not.*
>
> *But if I do, though ye believe not Me, believe the works: that ye may know, and believe, that the Father is in Me, and I in Him.*

If the Father is in you, you will do the same works that Jesus did. Jesus said, *"believe the works: that ye may know, and believe, that the Father is in Me..."*

Also in Mark 16:17-20, Jesus is speaking to the disciples:

*And these signs shall follow them that
believe; In My name shall they cast out
devils; they shall speak with new tongues;
They shall take up serpents; and if they
drink any deadly thing, it shall not hurt
them; they shall lay hands on the sick, and
they shall recover.'*

So then after the Lord had spoken unto
them, He was received up into heaven,
and sat on the right hand of God.

And they went forth, and preached
everywhere, the Lord working with them,
and confirming the word with signs
following. Amen.

conclusion

What more can we say? There is much, much more, but I
have only covered the essentials. The indwelling of the Holy Spirit
is a necessary step in the salvation process and before we have
received the indwelling of the Holy Spirit we are believing that we
will be saved. Now if you have not yet received the indwelling, do
not despair. Hold onto that faith and listen to God. He **promised**
in His Word that those who believe on Him **will be** saved. Hold
onto that promise and pray. The Holy Spirit WILL come. He has
promised it.

I am not saying that if you have not received the Holy
Spirit that you are condemned. If you are believing on Jesus for
salvation, then the Bible says you WILL BE saved. But, you *can*
have the "guarantee" now. Remember what Peter told the people
of Jerusalem in Acts 2:38-39:

> Then Peter said unto them, "*Repent, and be baptized every one of you in the name of Jesus Christ for the remission of sins, **and ye SHALL** receive the gift of the Holy Ghost.*
> *For **the promise** is unto you, and to your children, and to all that are afar off, even as many as the Lord our God shall call.*"

You *can* have the Holy Spirit now as a possession. You *can* have the quickening of your dead carnal body to a new spiritual body. You *can* have the indwelling of the Holy Spirit. You *can* have eternal life, right now, inside of you. You *can* have the kingdom of God right now.

We have shown that a person cannot lose their salvation once they have received the indwelling of the Holy Spirit. Also, we briefly looked at the importance and purpose of the Holy Ghost and that it is to continue the works that Jesus started.

We have also looked at how to know *when* we have the indwelling of the Holy Ghost. We looked at several ideas on the answer to this question and have shown where they do not line up with the Word. Also, we have shown where the Word indicates that spiritual revelation is the evidence of a person having the Holy Spirit and therefore the proof of salvation.

Finally, I can only repeat what Paul write in Ephesians 3:16-17:

> I pray that out of His glorious riches He may strengthen you with power through His Spirit in your inner being, so that Christ may dwell in your hearts through faith.

Three

RECEIVING HEALING

he following essay is written based on my own personal experience with actual true physical healings that were performed by the Holy Spirit. Some of these healings were instantaneous miracles where all symptoms of disease immediately disappeared. Other healings occurred gradually over a several-hour or several-day period of time.

There are several true personal stories in this book. I want to say that these are not fiction or exaggerations. These events truly happened exactly how I state them. God does not need me to exaggerate for Him.

Before someone can receive healing there is usually a need to first explain the Biblical basis for healing. First, they have to be reassured that healing is promised for them. This essay is based on the scriptures that I typically use. There are many, many more such scriptures; these are only the ones I have marked out in my Bible.

Too many people know too little about the Bible, yet a few things they do seem to know is that God *can* heal but *only if it is God's will* or that Paul had a "thorn of the flesh" that God did not heal, at least for a time, as if anyone should compare themselves with Paul.[24] I am going to show that physical bodily healing IS promised for those who believe.

This essay appears to be written in a step-by-step order, but please read the entire essay before you put it into practice.

Of course, this essay is not to take the place of proper medical care or advice of a doctor. There is nothing wrong with visiting physicians. In James 5:13-14, it is written:

> Is any among you afflicted? Let him pray.
> Is any merry? Let him sing psalms.
> Is any sick among you? Let him call for the elders of the church; and let them pray over him, **anointing him with oil** in the name of the Lord: and the prayer of faith SHALL save the sick, and the Lord SHALL raise him up.

There are some scholars who have taken this statement "anointing him with oil" to be medicine. There is nothing wrong with proper medical care or the advice of a doctor.

Now before I continue, I must say that the methodology of this essay is very mechanical. That is, I try to explain step by step how faith is developed for healing. Understand that this will help

---

[24] We will talk more about Paul's "thorn" later.

some people and be a hindrance for others. I have met many people who do not need to be shown "how it works." Just show them the scriptures in the Bible, they take God at His Word and believe it, and then the person receives the healing. Some others cannot seem to believe anything unless they understand the mechanics behind it. They have to know "how it works" in order to use it. This essay is aimed at helping these mechanically minded people. If you are not of that type, then perhaps the only value you will find here is the scripture references.

Base your Faith on God's Word

First you must know that there are many scriptures that promise healing. These scriptures should be the basis of your faith.

Everyone knows that Jesus was a healer. Even the Pharisees did not discount His works. But does Jesus heal today? I tell you that if Jesus healed two thousand years ago then he will do it now because Hebrews 13:8 says, **"Jesus Christ the same yesterday, and today, and forever"** and Malachi 3:6 says, **"For I am the LORD, I change not."** Therefore, we can safely say that the works that Jesus did 2000 years ago can be performed by Him today.

Additionally, the very nature of God is to heal. God called Himself a variety of names in the Old Testament besides Y-HW-H. Some of the other names He called Himself described His own Nature. For example, He is called Jehovah-Jireh which means *I am the Lord that provides.*[25] He also called Himself Jehovah-

---

[25] See Genesis 22:14 for the use of the title *Jehovah Jireh.*

Rapha which means *I am the Lord that heals thee*.[26] So it is in the nature of God, a God who does not change, to heal.

OK, so God heals, but is He willing to heal *me*? Yes, God does not give healing specially to one person over another. God treats all people equally. In Acts 10:34-35, Luke writes:

> Then Peter opened *his* mouth, and said,
> 'Of a truth I perceive that God is no respecter
> of persons: **but in every nation he that
> feareth Him, and worketh righteousness,
> is accepted with Him**.'

If one person receives healing by approaching God in a certain way and if another person approaches God in the same manner and spirit that the first person did, then the second will receive healing likewise. Romans 2:11 says, "For **God does not show favoritism**." And in Ephesians 6:9 Paul writes:

> And, ye masters, do the same things unto
> them, forbearing threatening: knowing that
> your Master also is in heaven; **neither is
> there partiality** with Him.

God does not change and God does not play favorites. It is written in Colossians 3:25, "But he that doeth wrong shall receive for the wrong which he hath done: and **there is no respect of persons**."[27]

---

[26] See Exodus 15:26, Isaiah 53:4, and Matthew 8:17 for descriptions of God as a healer, *Jehovah Rapha*.

[27] Deuteronomy 10:17 also says that God is not partial

Faith is the Approach to the Throne of God

Now, we have seen that God *can* heal and that healing is in the nature of God. Likewise, we have seen that God does not change and therefore, if we approach God in the same manner as another who has received then we MUST receive likewise. So, *how* do we approach? The approach to healing is always through faith.

Let me remind you that faith has nothing to do with the five senses. Faith could even be called a sixth sense, a spiritual sense. In fact in the case of healing, the five senses *may* run counter to faith. I have seen many people who are seeking after healing who visually look at their symptoms and if the symptom does not immediately get better, they lose faith. Or sometimes the symptoms get better for a few days, and then later get worse. They say something like, "*I thought for sure God would heal me!*" Clearly these people did not understand how faith works and therefore they opened the door for the disease to return. Here is an example of what one person wrote to me:

> I want this evil affliction to leave me. I want to have a healthy life. I hope someone will join me in prayer. To hear the Lord is a Healer right now is such a distressing statement for me because I can't understand why I have not been healed all these years and why I am allowed to suffer like I was still doing my old evils. Healing is the children's bread right? Why is it not being served to me? I know the Lord loves me but if only He could heal me. Please pray with me.

This is a perfect example of wrong thinking. The Lord God CAN heal anyone. The Lord WANTS to heal, it is in His NATURE. But God has processes that He has set in order and we

69

must follow them. Everyone *can* receive healing, they only have to *believe*. So, how do we believe?

Obtain a Mental Belief

As I have already stated in the previous chapter, there are two different kinds of belief, or faith, that we can talk about: a mental–psychological kind and a spiritual kind. The mental kind is the more common and occurs when we choose to hold fast to something in our mind. The spiritual can only be given by the Holy Spirit. Now remember, we are talking about believing things that we cannot verify with our five senses. If we can verify it with our five senses then it is not faith, but knowledge.

Remember, a person can be preached to, or read the Word, and say that they believe something in the Bible because it sounds good and makes sense. It is reasonable because it is the same message that we have heard since we were small kids. But do you believe it *truly*? Or is there a shadow of a doubt? Do you have a mental faith only or do you also have spiritual faith? **Spiritual faith for healing only comes through the Holy Spirit.**

Before the Holy Spirit can come, a person must first believe mentally. The Holy Spirit is not going to fall on an unrepentant sinner and *force* him to be saved *or to be healed*. First, develop a mental belief and then later, the Holy Spirit will come and give you the spiritual belief. I call this first step "getting your mind out of the way." The person who wishes to be healed must convince themselves *mentally* that God will give them *personally* what He promises in the scriptures *literally*. The person must rely totally and completely on the promises of God found in the scriptures, not on any change in physical symptoms. Once you

70

have done this, you now have a mental belief.

Now let us look at some scriptural examples of healings and draw some observations about them so that we might have something to base our faith on. In Matthew 4:23-24 it is written:

> And Jesus went about all Galilee, teaching in their synagogues, and preaching the gospel of the kingdom, and healing **ALL** manner of sickness and **ALL** manner of disease among the people.
> And His fame went throughout all Syria: and they brought unto Him **ALL** sick people that were taken with diverse diseases and torments, and those which were possessed with devils, and those which were lunatic, and those that had the palsy; **and He healed them**.

And in Matthew 12:15, it says, "But when Jesus knew *it*, He withdrew himself from thence: and great multitudes followed him, **and He healed them ALL**."

Also look at Matthew 8:16-17:

> When the even was come, they brought unto Him many that were possessed with devils:
> and He [Jesus] cast out the spirits with *His* word, **and healed ALL that were sick**:
> that it might be fulfilled which was spoken by Esaias [Isaiah] the prophet, saying, "*Himself took our infirmities, and bare our sicknesses*."

In Mark 6:56, it says:

> And whithersoever He [Jesus] entered, into villages, or cities, or country, they laid the

> sick in the streets, and besought Him that
> they might touch if it were but the border of
> His garment: and **as many as touched Him
> were made whole**.

I think you might start to notice from these examples that Jesus healed ALL people of ALL diseases and cast out ALL demons of **people who were *brought to Him*.**

Right away some people will think about an example where Jesus heals only one person out of many. An example where there were many people sick and Jesus walks up to one, the one who had faith, and healed only that one and left. But that is exactly the point. There is a difference between the times when Jesus *went to* someone to heal them, and when the sick *came to* Jesus. When Jesus went to someone, He sometimes only went to one person – the one who had faith. On the other hand, when WE come to Jesus, He heals ALL people of ALL sickness, and casts out ALL demons.

Our coming to Him IS the exercise of faith. Here are a few more examples, in Matthew 14:35-36:

> And when the men of that place had
> knowledge of Him [Jesus], they sent out into
> all that country round about, and brought unto
> Him ALL that were diseased;
> And besought Him that they might only
> touch the hem of his garment: and **as many
> as touched** were made perfectly whole.

Also, Luke 4:40-41:

> Now when the sun was setting, all they
> that had any sick with diverse diseases
> brought them unto Him; and He laid His
> hands **on every one of them**, and healed
> them.

> And devils also came out of many, crying out, and saying, *"Thou art Christ the Son of God."*
>
> And He rebuking *them* suffered them not to speak: for they knew that He was Christ.

Before we say that these healings are *only* done by Jesus, let us look at Acts of the Apostles 5:12-16:

> And **by the hands of the apostles** were many signs and wonders wrought among the people; (and they were all with one accord in Solomon's porch.
>
> And of the rest durst no man join himself to them: but the people magnified them.
>
> And believers were the more added to the Lord, multitudes both of men and women.)
>
> Insomuch that they brought forth the sick into the streets, and laid *them* on beds and couches, that at the least the shadow of Peter passing by might overshadow some of them.
>
> There came also a multitude *out* of the cities round about unto Jerusalem, bringing sick folks, and them which were vexed with unclean spirits: **and they were healed every one**.

The power of God will heal ALL people that have faith and approach Him to be healed. But *why* does He heal us? Because healing is the earnest of life. What do you mean by *earnest*? In Ephesians 1:13-14, Paul writes:

> In whom ye also trusted, after that ye heard the word of truth, the gospel of your salvation: in whom also after that ye believed, ye were sealed with that Holy Spirit of promise, which is the **earnest** of our inheritance until the redemption of the

purchased possession, unto the praise of his glory.

This word "earnest" is sometimes translated "guarantee" or "down payment" and in Greek is the word αρραβων. Sickness is the first fruit or earnest or proof of death. Likewise, healing is the first fruit or earnest or proof or guarantee of life. It is like Jesus is saying *"I am going to die on the cross for you so that you might be saved and go to heaven with Me, and to prove it to you, I will give you a down payment for this future life in the form of healing."*

The atoning blood of Jesus was for BOTH salvation AND healing. Let us read the prophecy concerning Jesus in Isaiah 53 *carefully*:

> Who hath believed our report? and to whom is the arm of the LORD revealed?
> For He shall grow up before Him as a tender plant, and as a root out of a dry ground: He hath no form nor comeliness; and when we shall see Him, *there is* no beauty that we should desire Him.
> He is despised and rejected of men; a man of sorrows, and acquainted with grief: and we hid as it were *our* faces from Him; He was despised, and we esteemed Him not.
> **Yet He Himself bore our sicknesses, and He carried our pains**: yet we did esteem Him stricken, smitten of God, and afflicted.
> But **He *was* wounded for our transgressions, *He was* bruised for our iniquities: the chastisement of our peace *was* upon Him; and by His stripes we are healed**.
> All we like sheep have gone astray; we have turned every one to his own way; and

the LORD hath laid on Him the iniquity of us all.

He was oppressed, and He was afflicted, yet He opened not His mouth: He is brought as a lamb to the slaughter, and as a sheep before her shearers is dumb, so He openeth not His mouth.

He was taken from prison and from judgment: and who shall declare His generation?

For He was cut off out of the land of the living: for the transgression of My people was He stricken.

And He made His grave with the wicked, and with the rich in His death; because He had done no violence, neither *was any* deceit in His mouth.

Yet it pleased the LORD to bruise Him; He hath put *Him* to grief: when thou shalt make His soul an offering for sin, He shall see *His* seed, He shall prolong *His* days, and the pleasure of the LORD shall prosper in His hand.

He shall see of the travail of His soul, *and* shall be satisfied: by His knowledge shall my righteous servant justify many; **for He shall bear their iniquities.**

Therefore will I divide Him *a portion* with the great, and He shall divide the spoil with the strong; because He hath poured out His soul unto death: and He was numbered with the transgressors; and He bare the sin of many, **and made intercession for the transgressors.**

Pray in Faith

Now we are developing something here. We have seen that God *can* heal and that healing is in the nature of God. Likewise, we have seen that God does not change and honors any person who approaches Him in His preordained pattern, therefore, if we approach God in the same manner as another who has received then we MUST receive likewise. Also we have seen that Jesus will heal ALL people that have faith and approach Him to be healed. We have seen that before the Holy Spirit can come with revelation knowledge a person must first believe mentally. And we have looked at some scriptures to boost our mental faith. We are convincing ourselves mentally.

Next, we must pray and ask God for the healing. If we believe it is a demon, then cast it out. The thing to remember is that there is no time element with prayer. The moment that you pray, your pray is heard and the floodgates of heaven are opened. Of course there are some things that can block your prayer, such as being unrepentant, unforgiveness, or a lack of faith, among others. But, take care of those issues first, then there will be nothing to block your prayer and you WILL be healed.

Also, be specific in what you pray for. Pray for EXACTLY what you want and believe that you will receive EXACTLY what you ask for. Psalms 27:4 says, "**One *thing* have I desired of the LORD, that will I seek after…**" Fix in your mind what you desire. Pray for that exact thing and believe you receive that exact thing. Seek after this one thing until it is manifest in your life.

Now, the promise from God that is written in His Word is that if you pray you WILL get healed.

In James 5:13-16, it is written:

> Is any among you afflicted? Let him pray.
> Is any merry? Let him sing psalms.
> **Is any sick among you? Let him call
> for the elders of the church; and let them
> pray over him, anointing him with oil in
> the name of the Lord: and the prayer of
> faith SHALL save the sick, and the Lord
> SHALL raise him up**; and if he have
> committed sins, they shall be forgiven him.
> Confess *your* faults one to another, and
> pray one for another, that ye may be healed.
> The effectual fervent prayer of a righteous
> man availeth much.

This is the Word of God now. It said, "...the prayer of faith SHALL save the sick, and the Lord SHALL raise him up..." It does not say that the Lord *might* raise him up. It does not say the Lord will raise him up *only if He is in the mood.* It does not say the Lord will think about it first and *then say, "No."*

It says, "**The prayer of faith SHALL save the sick, and the Lord SHALL raise him up!**"

In John 14:13, Jesus says,

> *And whatsoever ye shall ask in My name,
> that will I do, that the Father may be glorified
> in the Son.*

Also in Luke 11:9-13, Jesus says:

> *And I say unto you, **Ask, and it shall
> be given you; seek, and ye shall find;
> knock, and it shall be opened unto
> you.***
> *   **For every one that asketh**

receiveth; and he that seeketh findeth; and to him that knocketh it shall be opened.

If a son shall ask bread of any of you that is a father, will he give him a stone?

Or if he ask a fish, will he for a fish give him a serpent?

Or if he shall ask an egg, will he offer him a scorpion?

If ye then, being evil, know how to give good gifts unto your children: how much more shall your heavenly Father give the Holy Spirit to them that ask Him?

In Mark 11:20-24, it is written,

And in the morning, as they passed by, they saw the fig tree dried up from the roots.

And Peter calling to remembrance said unto Him, *"Master, behold, the fig tree which Thou cursed is withered away."*

And Jesus answering saith unto them, *"Have faith in God.*

For verily I say unto you, That whosoever shall say unto this mountain, "Be thou removed, and be thou cast into the sea";

and shall not doubt in his heart, but shall believe that those things which he said shall come to pass; he shall have whatsoever he said.

Therefore I say unto you, **What things soever ye desire, when ye pray, believe that ye receive them, and ye shall have them.** *"*

At the end of Mark 16:17-18, Jesus issues the great commission to spread the gospel to all the world and says:

And these signs shall follow them that believe; In My name shall they cast out devils; they shall speak with new tongues; they shall take up serpents; and if they drink any deadly thing, it shall not hurt them; **they SHALL lay hands on the sick, and they SHALL recover.**

Again, this is the Word of God. This is Jesus speaking! He said, *"They SHALL recover."* Jesus does not say that they *might* recover. It does not say they *sometimes* recover. It says, ***"They SHALL recover!"***

How To Pray

Some people have asked me to explain *exactly* how to pray for healing. They are not sure if they should beg at the feet of Jesus or demand to be healed. On one hand it sounds like we have no faith and on the other it seems like we are ordering God around.

I am not here to tell anyone how to pray to God, but I will tell you **what I do** and **what has been successful for me**. Remember, if we approach God the same way that others have who have received, then we should receive likewise because God does not play favorites.

How I pray can be divided into at least three distinct parts. First, we ask God for healing. We do not command God. Neither do we beg, but we ask God to grant us healing based upon HIS

PROMISE that He gave us. We are only asking for God to give us what God has already promised to give us.

I say something along these lines, *"Lord, in your Word, I see that **all** people who approach You in faith are healed. Lord, according to your Word, I know that **You are a healer**. Lord, according to your Word, I know that You **can** heal. Lord, according to your Word, I know that **it is in Your nature to heal**. You called Yourself **Jehova-Rapha**. Lord, according to your Word, I know that You **want** to heal."*

I continue, *"You said, 'Ask, and it shall be given you; seek, and ye shall find; knock, and it shall be opened unto you.' So, I am coming to You, Lord, **by faith in the promises found in Your Word** and asking You to heal me as You have promised. You said in your word, 'the prayer of faith SHALL save the sick, and the Lord SHALL raise him up.' I am basing my faith totally and completely on **Your promise found in Your Word**. I will not place my faith in any change in my symptoms, but only in your Word."*

The second step is not really a prayer at all but is really speaking directly to the sickness or demon. I turn my attention to the sickness or the demon and command it to leave. I say, *"Sickness [Demon], according to the promise of God found in the book of James, you must leave. It says, 'The prayer of faith SHALL save the sick, and the Lord SHALL raise him up.' I have prayed in faith and therefore you have **no choice** but to leave this body. I am speaking on the authority of the Lord Jesus Christ. Sickness, I rebuke you. Sickness, I cast you out in the name of the Lord Jesus Christ. You have no choice but to leave. You have no authority here. You are commanded to leave in the name of the Lord Jesus Christ."*

Now, I have seen people who will scream this and get very

excited and emotional. That is all right to do that, but it is not necessary. It is not emotion that is scaring the sickness or demon into leaving, but it is the power of the name of Jesus being used in faith. Of course, for some people getting worked up or emotional helps to increase their faith.

The third part of my prayer is praise. I worship God and thank Him for healing me. I praise God's name and CLAIM the healing. I say things like, "*According to Thy will and according to Thy Word, I am healed!*" and, "*I am healed according to Thy will Lord!*" and "*Thank you for Healing me, Lord Jesus!*" I repeat scriptures. I say, "*The Bible says, 'What things soever ye desire, when ye pray, believe that ye receive them, and ye shall have them' and I believe that I receive O, Lord!*"

Do You Want to Believe?

Now if you WANT to believe, but think maybe your faith is insufficient, then first pray for the faith and the Lord will provide that also. In Mark 9:23-24:

> Jesus said unto him, '*If thou canst believe, all things are possible to him that believeth.*'
> And straightway the father of the child cried out, and said with tears, '*Lord, I believe; help thou mine unbelief.*'

And we find that Jesus DID help his unbelief, and the child was healed. You see sometimes we want to believe so bad, but we don't know if what little faith we have is enough. Will God honor this little bit of faith that I have?

Hebrews 2:2 says:

> Looking unto Jesus, **the author and finisher of _our_ faith**; who for the joy that was set before Him endured the cross, despising the shame, and is set down at the right hand of the throne of God.

God provides our faith. We can never believe enough mentally. We must have a spiritual faith, and that is provided by God alone.

Obtain a Spiritual Belief

Now we have completed the first few steps. We have a mental belief that God will take away our infirmity and we have prayed and asked God to honor His Word and His promise to us. Of course the mind is very tricky. There is probably some shadow of a doubt lurking in the back of our mind. Is this real? Is this _really_ going to work? Will God honor me when I am a sinner? What have I done for God? These thoughts, jumping in and out of our heads, come from two different places. Some are attacks of the Devil. The Devil has many thousands of years practice at disrupting prayer and faith.

Other times people sincerely have doubt in their own mind. They have little or no experience with faith so there is uncertainty. In either case, you mind gets in the way. You have to clear your mind of these doubts, uncertainties, and attacks of the Devil before your faith can rise up.

Do not worry about mental attacks. Do not pay any attention to them. Do not pay any attention to your five senses. Focus on the Word. Do not consider or look at anything but the promise of God. Keep your mind's eye on the promise found in the scriptures only. Pray, pray, and pray some more. Meditate only on those scriptures. Remember to CLAIM your healing. Constantly repeat OUT LOUD, "*I am healed according to Thy will Lord!*" and "*Thank you for Healing me, Lord Jesus!*" What you are actually doing is trying to get your mind "out of the way" so that the Holy Spirit can come.

Do this for as long as it takes. Sometimes it takes a few minutes, sometimes several hours. If you have to take a break and pick up the next day, OK, but never leave this subject until you receive the blessing. Do not give up early – pray for as long as it takes. In Luke 11:5-8, it is written:

> And He [Jesus] said unto them, "*Which of you shall have a friend, and shall go unto him at midnight, and say unto him, 'Friend, lend me three loaves; for a friend of mine in his journey is come to me, and I have nothing to set before him?'*
>
> *And he from within shall answer and say, 'Trouble me not: the door is now shut, and my children are with me in bed; I cannot rise and give thee.'*
>
> *I say unto you, Though he will not rise and give him, because he is his friend, yet* **because of the man's boldness** *he will rise and give him as many as he needeth.*"

After a time, your mind will "get out of the way," that small shadow of a doubt will leave, and the Holy Spirit will come and give you spiritual faith. When that happens your body may or may not still have the physical manifestations of the sickness. The disease or ailment may leave instantaneously, or it may not. There may be some physical sign of the healing or there maybe not.

But regardless of the condition of your body, you will KNOW, without any doubt, down in the depths of your spirit, that you are healed. This is revelation knowledge – the true spirit of faith that can only be granted by the Holy Spirit. It will not matter what your eyes see before you, you will KNOW that you are healed.

Hold fast to that revelation and if the healing was not instantaneous then after a time the body WILL respond. Understand that the Devil will start to attack you badly but rebuke him using the Word. Remember Abraham who did not consider (look at) his age or the deadness of Sarah's womb but only considered (looked at) the promise of God. It is not that he denied that he was old – he knew he was old – but he looked at the promise of God anyhow. He held fast to the promise – God's Word. He STARED at the promise.

Keep holding onto that blessed revelation that you are healed. Do not let your mind get back "in the way." Do not listen to the evil one. It is fine and all right to check and see if your symptoms are still there, but do not look at them to prop up your faith. Your faith is **only** in God's Word.

Now when you are done, you have prayed, you have received spiritual faith, you have received physical healing, then thank the Lord for the great work He has done.

Praying for Children

Mark 9:17-24, tells a story of a man who brings his son to Jesus to be healed. Jesus tells the father of the child, *"If thou canst believe, all things are possible to him that believeth."*

Notice that Jesus speaks to the father, not to the child who is sick. When we pray for children who are young, the faith of the person praying or a parent can stand in for the child. Once, the child is healed let them know what has happened and they will accept it.

About ten years ago, my oldest son was very sick with an ear infection. He was about four years old at the time. It was the middle of the night and he was howling in pain. It was the weekend and our local hospital was notorious for their six-hour weekend lines at the emergency room, so I thought it better to take him to the family doctor in the morning. Meanwhile, I crawled into his bed with him and started to pray for his healing. I knew that it would be my faith only that would reach out and touch the hem of Jesus' garment. I prayed continually for several hours until my mind got out of the way and my faith rose up. My son had been howling and whimpering in pain the whole time. All of a sudden I felt a force like two lightening bolts fly out of my chest, down each arm and into his body. His body physically bounced vertically up into the air, off the bed. He bounced several inches from this force.

Then there was a perfect calm and silence on the room. My son was instantaneously and completely healed. He was not howling, moaning or whimpering anymore. There was silence.

He rolled over and looked at me and said, "*Daddy, what happened?*"

I said, "*You were healed.*"

He said, "*OK,*" rolled over, and fell back to sleep.

The next morning he was up and playing like he was never ill. Everything was back to normal. Children typically do not backslide back into sickness because they accept the words of their parents unconditionally. My son believed what I told him was truth. We should do the same to our Father.

Healing Being Blocked

Another thing to note is that sickness comes SOMETIMES because of unbelief or sin. David said, "Before I was afflicted, I went astray."[28] And Psalm 107:17 says, "Fools because of their transgression, and because of their iniquities, are afflicted." So we must repent of our sin or unbelief BEFORE we can receive healing.

But this is not ALWAYS the case. Only sometimes. Other times people become sick who did not "go astray." There may or may not be a sin that caused the illness. In John 9:1-3, it is written:

> And as *Jesus* passed by, He saw a man which was blind from *his* birth. And His disciples asked Him, saying, *"Master, who did sin, this man, or his parents, that he was born blind?"*
>
> Jesus answered, *"Neither hath this man sinned, nor his parents: but that the works of God should be made manifest in him."*

Do not get hung up on some past sins if you have them, just repent and ask forgiveness for them first, that is all.

In addition to asking for forgiveness of your sins, you must forgive others. UNFORGIVENESS is the NUMBER ONE thing that can block a person from receiving healing. Remember salvation and healing are closely linked and the same rules apply to both in many ways. In Matthew 9:2-5, it is written:

> And, behold, they brought to Him [Jesus] a man sick of the palsy, lying on a bed: and Jesus seeing their faith said unto the sick of the palsy; *"Son, be of good cheer; thy sins be*

---

[28] David says this in Psalm 119:67.

forgiven thee."

And, behold, certain of the scribes said within themselves, "*This man blasphemeth.*"

And Jesus knowing their thoughts said, *"Wherefore think ye evil in your hearts? For whether is easier, to say, 'Thy sins be forgiven thee'; or to say, 'Arise, and walk?' "*

When describing The Lord's Prayer, look at how much emphasis Jesus places on forgiving others. Matthew 6:8,12,14-15 reads:

8 Be not ye therefore like unto them: for your Father knoweth what things ye have need of, before ye ask Him.

12 And forgive us our debts, as we forgive our debtors.

14 For if ye forgive men their trespasses, your heavenly Father will also forgive you:

15 But if ye forgive not men their trespasses, neither will your Father forgive your trespasses.

In all clarity, Jesus explains the close link between forgiving others and having your own prayers answered in Mark 11:24-26:

Therefore I say unto you, what things soever ye desire, when ye pray, believe that ye receive them, and ye shall have them.

And when ye stand praying, forgive, *if ye have ought against any: that your Father also which is in heaven may forgive you your trespasses.*

But if ye do not forgive, neither will your

Father which is in heaven forgive your
trespasses.

So, we see clearly by Jesus' example, we must let go of ALL unforgiveness we have. If we are holding a grudge against someone else, LET IT GO.

Paul's Thorn in the Flesh

It is well known that Paul had a "thorn in the flesh" and that God did not remove that "thorn" when Paul prayed. 2nd Corinthians 12:7-8 describes Paul's condition. Paul says:

> And lest I should be exalted above measure through the abundance of the revelations, **there was given to me a thorn in the flesh, the messenger of Satan to buffet me**, lest I should be exalted above measure.
> For this thing I besought the Lord thrice, that it might depart from me.

So many people know so little about the Bible, yet they seem to "know" that God did not answer Paul's prayer. People like to use Paul's thorn as an excuse for not receiving healing. "*Well, I prayed and I didn't get healed, I guess I'm just like Paul,*" they think. Do not let that thought enter your head. That is a lie of the Devil.

Paul's prayer was answered, but not in the way that people think. I will address the topic of how that prayer was answered in another essay[29], but for now, I want to focus on this "thorn."

---

[29] An essay that deals with this issue will be in my next book.

The standard interpretation is that Paul's thorn was an infection in his eyes. In Paul's writings, he dictated to a scribe. But Paul always wrote a few lines, usually the last few lines, of the letter so that people would know that it was an authentic letter from Paul. For example, in Thessalonians 3:17-18, the last few lines of the epistle, Paul writes:

> The salutation of Paul **with mine own hand, which is the token in every epistle**: so I write.
> The grace of our Lord Jesus Christ *be* with you all. Amen.

In these few lines, Paul sometimes says his writing was large. In Galatians 6:11, He says:

> Ye see how large a letter I have written unto you with mine own hand.

We do not know if he meant that his letter was too long, or that his characters were bigger than normal. I personally believe that he meant exactly what he said, that he wrote a longer than normal letter. Now, we do not know because the original epistles are gone, we only have copies, but scholars say that he meant that his characters were very big. They argue that this is because his eyesight was so bad. They use Galatians 4:13-15 to justify this, Paul writes:

> Ye know how through infirmity of the flesh
> I preached the gospel unto you at the first.[30]
> And my temptation which was in my flesh
> ye despised not, nor rejected; but received
> me as an angel of God, *even* as Christ Jesus.
> Where is then the blessedness ye spake

---

[30] Paul may have preached while being sick "at the first" but he certainly never complained of any sickness later on. Galatians was Paul's first letter being written in AD 48 and it appears here that he is no longer sick for he uses the past tense.

of? For I bear you record, that, if *it had been*
possible, ye would have plucked out your
own eyes, and have given them to me.

And how did his eyesight become poor? He was exposed
to a blinding light from God which he never really recovered from,
according to these scholars. So, they actually say that **God caused
Paul to be sick and then God refused to heal him.** This line of
thinking does not line up with scripture at all.

First, let me say that in no place in the Bible is the term
"thorn" used to depict sickness. Numbers 33:55 says:
But if ye will not drive out **the inhabitants
of the land** from before you; then it shall
come to pass, that those which ye let remain
of them *shall be* **pricks in your eyes, and
thorns in your sides**, and shall vex you in
the land wherein ye dwell.

And Joshua 23:13 says:
Know for a certainty that the LORD your
God will no more drive out *any of* these
nations from before you; but they shall be
snares and traps unto you, and **scourges in
your sides, and thorns in your eyes**, until
ye perish from off this good land which the
LORD your God hath given you.

So, we see that the "thorn" is always a person or a group of
people that antagonize.

Second, let us look at the next line in Paul's description:
**there was given to me a thorn in the
flesh, the messenger of Satan to buffet
me**, lest I should be exalted above measure.

Paul says that it was a "**messenger of Satan.**" A "messenger" (angelos) could be an angelic being or a person, but it is certainly not a disease.[31]

Third, we see that this "messenger," who was antagonizing Paul, was "buffeting" him. To buffet is to hit repeatedly. This does not sound like a disease at all. In fact why would Paul say, "*I am being repeatedly hit by this 'demon,'*" instead of just saying, "*I got hurt eyes?*" Now remember, Paul is one of the most open, clear and plain of all the prophets, yet people think what he says here is in some kind of a code? [32] No. What Paul CLEARLY says is that he is being antagonized repeatedly by a messenger of Satan.

In 1st Corinthians 4:11-13, Paul lists the buffetings by Satan that he has been suffering from. He says:

> **Even unto this present hour we both hunger, and thirst, and are naked, and are buffeted**, and have no certain dwelling place;
> And labor, working with our own hands: **being reviled… being persecuted…being defamed…we are made as the filth of the world,** *and are* the off scouring of all things unto this day.

So here is a list of Paul's buffetings, and I do not see any sign of a sickness anywhere on the list. Now, why is that? I guess

---

[31] See my essay *God in a Man* for a more detailed explanation of the Greek word *angelos* and how it can mean either an angelic being or a human messenger.

[32] In fact, the majority of Paul's writings were responses to questions from the churches. Paul was turned to as an authority who would clear up misunderstandings.

it just slipped his mind. No. It is not listed because Paul's "thorn in the flesh" had NOTHING to do with illness.[33]

Sorry, to beat this up, but I get upset when people deny the power of God. People mention Paul's thorn and say, *"Oh, sometimes God says 'No' when a person prays to be healed, that's why I'm not healed."* That is completely false. God **never** says "N*o*" to **healing**.[34] It is amazing that these people can deny the simple and direct Word of God found **throughout the entire Bible** that says God heals and point at this one scripture that really says nothing about sickness, and then they twist it. If you did not receive your healing then there may be some other reason, but it is not God saying "*No*." God heals!

Now I am not pointing this out to try and put people down who did not receive a healing. I **want** people to be healed and will do anything I can to help achieve this goal. It is only the Devil who is putting some kind of a block in front of the healing. This is who we need to be angry with.

If the above three reasons do not sway you, let me give you one more. A personal testimony. I had an infection in *my* eyes. I would wake up some mornings with my eyes sealed shut from the gunk pouring out. So, I prayed for healing. Now, I have been healed by the power of God more times than I can count but this time I prayed different. I prayed, *"Lord, if Paul's thorn in the flesh was a sickness, then not only do I want You to NOT heal me, but make my eyes worse. If it was something other than a sickness then please heal my eyes, Lord."* I had to have reassurance. I had

---

[33] *1st* and *2nd Corinthians* were both written around AD 56, probably from Philippi or Ephesus (see Acts 20:1-6) before Paul's first imprisonment in Rome in AD 60. Paul later wrote *Ephesians, Philippians, Colossians, Philemon, 1st* and *2nd Timothy,* and *Titus.* He does not mention any continuing or past eye problem, nor does he complain of any sickness in any of these letters.

[34] God may say "no" to some other request, but God NEVER says "no" to a request for healing.

to know without a shadow of doubt. I had to have the Truth, not by being mentally convinced, but direct from God.

Some people think that kind of a prayer is dangerous, but I did it anyway. Now, I did not sit on the fence thinking *maybe I'll wait and see*, but leaned completely on the promises of the Word of God in the Bible. The promises that said that *I would be healed*. I did not wait to see if God would *make up His mind*. No, I believed fully that I *would* be healed. I prayed for this healing the same that I would pray for any other. Stand on the Word, get my mind out of the way, and receive.

Then, the Lord spoke to me and I *was* healed. Every bit of that yellow ooze from my eyes disappeared that very day. I had that infection for over three weeks and it had been getting worse and worse everyday. Now, it was completely and totally gone.

This healing was no different than any other I have received. Just like all the others, the Devil tried to attack and bring the sickness back. The Devil tries to get you to doubt God's Word. After two weeks I did not have one bit of the symptoms, then one morning I woke up and it was back. I knew it immediately because it itches. You cannot stop thinking about it because you constantly want to scratch. Later that afternoon I got upset and started to yell out and rebuke it in the name of Jesus. I screamed out about forty times. The symptoms stayed for the rest of the day, but I knew that demon would have no choice but to leave. The next morning I woke up and it was completely gone again. It never returned.

Many times this happens, the Devil tries to bring a symptom back to make you doubt God's Word. Once you lose faith, it opens the door for the full return of the sickness.

I do not care how much someone wants to rely on Paul's "thorn" to justify why they didn't get healed or why they do not have healing in their congregation. The fact of the matter is that God heals and that God does not say "*No*" to healing. God wants to heal you!

Block the Return of the Sickness

Now get full of the Holy Spirit to prevent the sickness' or demon's return. Never open the door to Satan. Never stop praying, never stop reading the Word, and never stop seeking after holiness, purity, and righteousness. In Luke 11:24-26, Jesus says:

> *When the unclean spirit is gone out of a man, he walketh through dry places, seeking rest; and finding none, he [the demon] saith, "I will return unto my house whence I came out."*
>
> *And when he cometh, he findeth it swept and garnished. Then goeth he, and taketh to him seven other spirits more wicked than himself; and they enter in, and dwell there: and the last state of that man is worse than the first.*

If you have not obtained the Holy Spirit in your heart and kept a continual filling, then you have left an open door for the demon or the sickness to return. In John 5:14, it says:

> Afterward Jesus findeth him in the temple, and said unto him, '*Behold, thou art made whole: sin no more, lest a worse thing come unto thee.*'

94

Conclusion

If you are sick right now, you can place what you have read into practice, right now. Of course, I want to caution you. With God all things are possible and easy, but with man there can be difficulties. I see too many people try and fail, they give up too early. When the Devil comes into their mind they lose faith. Be prepared, the Devil is going to fight you over every inch of ground. Read the essay again. Know those healing scriptures, and know that they are the true Word of God.

Now, before you start praying, analyze yourself. Do you have anything that would block your healing? Is there anyone that you have not forgiven? Do you have anything that needs to be made right? Take care of these things first. I assure you that if you do not, the Devil will surely use them to attack you mentally and try to block your faith when you sit down to pray. Make things right first. Many times all it takes is a phone call.

Then, remember how to pray. First, we ask God for healing. We ask God to grant us healing based upon HIS PROMISE that He gave us. We are asking God to give us what He has already promised to give us.

Say something along these lines, "*Lord, in your Word, I see that **all** people who approach You in faith are healed. Lord, according to your Word, I know that **You are a healer**. Lord, according to your Word, I know that You **can** heal. Lord, according to your Word, I know that **it is in Your nature to heal**. You called Yourself **Jehova-Rapha**. Lord, according to your Word, I know that You **want** to heal.*"

Continue with, "*You said, 'Ask, and it shall be given you; seek, and ye shall find; knock, and it shall be opened unto you.'*

*So, I am coming to You, Lord, **by faith in the promises found in Your Word** and asking You to heal me as You have promised. You said, 'The prayer of faith SHALL save the sick, and the Lord SHALL raise him up.' I am basing my faith totally and completely on **Your promise found in Your Word.** I will not place my faith in any change in my symptoms, but only in your Word.* "

Next, turn your attention to the sickness or the demon and command it to leave. Say, "S*ickness [Demon], according to the promise of God found in the book of James, you must leave. It says, 'The prayer of faith SHALL save the sick, and the Lord SHALL raise him up.' I have prayed in faith and therefore you have **no choice** but to leave this body. I am speaking on the authority of the Lord Jesus Christ. Sickness, I rebuke you. Sickness, I cast you out in the name of the Lord Jesus Christ. You have no choice but to leave. You have no authority here. You are commanded to leave in the name of the Lord Jesus Christ.*"

Then, worship God and thank Him for healing you. Praise God's name and CLAIM the healing. Say things like, "*According to Thy will and according to Thy Word, I am healed!*" or "*I am healed according to Thy will Lord!*" or "*Thank you for Healing me, Lord Jesus!*" or "*Jesus said, '**What things soever ye desire, when ye pray, believe that ye receive them, and ye shall have them**' and I believe that I receive O, Lord!*"

Do this as long as it takes. Remember that you have only a mental faith and you are waiting for the Holy Spirit to provide the spiritual faith. For some people it only takes a few moments for them to get their "mind out of the way," for others it can take hours or days. Never give up! Pray as long as it takes! God will provide! He has promised it!

Of course, it is perfectly alright to check your symptoms but do not put any faith in them. Your faith is totally and completely in God's Word. Sometimes the healing will be a process. You might start getting a little better initially. You might start feeling better. It is very tempting to fix in your mind that, "*Look! It's working! I'm starting to get healed!*" I urge you not to do this, because what you are actually doing is starting to rely on your feelings instead of your faith in the Word. This is a big mistake. You must rely on your sixth sense not your five senses.

What I have seen is that people turn their attention away from the Word and towards their feelings, then, if there is a negative change in the feelings or symptoms, they lose faith. Do not do that. It is alright to check your symptoms, but keep your faith totally and completely on God's Word. You will be healed.

God bless you and I pray that all will be healed, whoever has need and asks of the Lord. I pray that the Lord gives you out of the abundance of His heart.

Four

ON THIS ROCK

he format of this essay is noticeably different than others I have written. In this one, I am surveying five different interpretations of Matthew 16:18. I am *attempting* to give an equal explanation of all five in order that we might see the root behind these interpretations and how certain ideas influence a broader range of Christian thought. Let us start out by reading Matthew 16:13-19:

> 13 When Jesus came into the coasts of Caesarea Philippi, He asked His disciples, saying, *"Whom do men say that I, the Son of man, am?"*
>
> 14 And they said, *"Some say that Thou art John the Baptist: some, Elias; and others, Jeremias, or one of the prophets."*

¹⁵ He saith unto them, *"But whom say ye that I am?"*

¹⁶ And Simon Peter answered and said, "Thou art the Christ, the Son of the living God."

¹⁷ And Jesus answered and said unto him, *"Blessed art thou, Simon Bar-jona: for flesh and blood hath not revealed it unto thee, but My Father which is in heaven.*

¹⁸ And I say also unto thee, That thou art Peter, and upon this rock I will build My church; and the gates of hell shall not prevail against it.

¹⁹ And I will give unto thee the keys of the kingdom of heaven: and whatsoever thou shalt bind on earth shall be bound in heaven: and whatsoever thou shalt loose on earth shall be loosed in heaven."

Peter is the Rock

By the year 1500, the Roman Catholic Church had been discouraging people from reading the Bible for over one thousand years. Instead, the Church dictated the meaning of scriptures to the public. Most people could not read anyway, and interpretation of scripture took years of formal training and indoctrination in church schools. And besides, the public saw that every scripture was clearly understood by the Church because the Church presented one uniform meaning of the scriptures openly and readily.

"Why should I check scriptures myself, if a highly trained and honorable, high ranking member of the clergy is eager to explain them to me?" some might say.

The interpretation of Matthew 16:18 presented by the Catholic Church to the public was clear.[35] The Church interpreted "this rock" to be Peter in the scripture *"Thou art Peter, and upon this rock I will build my church."* One of the reasons this interpretation would make perfect sense is that Peter and rock have similar spellings and sounds in many European languages. For example, in Spanish Peter is translated *Pedro* and rock is translated *piedra.* In Greek, Peter is *Petros* and rock is *petra.* Likewise, in Latin Peter is *Petrus* and rock is *petram.* The similarity in the spelling and sounds of the two words is too close to be a coincidence, Catholic scholars would argue. If Jesus did not want people to be confused, He would have used different words. Jesus could have called Peter by his real name –Simon. Or instead of "rock", Jesus could have said pebble, stone, or boulder. But He didn't. For the Catholic Church, the close relationship between the two words, "Peter" and "rock", shows that Peter is the foundation stone of the church. This fact was useful for the Church as it was used as scriptural support to establish Roman authority.

In Matthew 28:19-20, Jesus issued the great commission:
Go ye therefore, and teach all nations, baptizing them in the name of the Father, and of the Son, and of the Holy Ghost: teaching them to observe all things whatsoever I have commanded you: and, lo, I am with you always, even unto the end of the world.

---

[35] Do not think that I am against the Catholic Church (or any other denomination) because of these comments about the position of the Church in the 1500's. All this information can be found in any decent college level History textbook on the Reformation.

This order to spread the good news of the gospel to "every nation" across the globe was one reason there were many different Christian churches spread throughout the nations even in the early years of the religion. Another reason was that persecution of Christians forced many to leave their homelands for foreign soil. As a result, many disciples spread out and formed churches great distances apart. Peter and Paul founded the church at Rome and Peter became the first bishop of Rome. When Peter died, his bones were buried in the catacombs of Rome. St. Peter's Basilica was later built on top of these same catacombs. The position of the Catholic Church is that the only *real* Church that has authority is built scripturally upon the *rock of Peter* and literally St. Peter's Basilica is built directly on top of Peter's bones. In fact, in giant gold letters around the base of Michelangelo's dome at St. Peter's Basilica are inscribed the words, "Thou art Peter, and upon this rock I will build my church."

In the formative years of the Church, the bishop of Rome claimed authority over all other Christian churches using the scriptural strength of Peter. Matthew 16:18 is one of those scriptures. Over a long period of time, the idea of the bishop of Rome being the head of the entire Church gradually evolved. This probably started around 476 with the fall of the Roman empire. The power void created by the fall allowed the Roman Catholic bishops to increase their power over the provinces. Between 1073 and 1303, the papacy reached the summit of its power. The bishop of Rome became something more: a Pope. Pope Innocent III (1198-1216) claimed the title of "supreme sovereign over the church and the world." Catholics would eventually say that if the current Pope is speaking, then that is the same as if Peter was speaking.

The Pope used this authority to establish "tradition based" elements in the church. These elements were not necessarily in the Bible, but came to have the same standing as other items that were Bible based.

The Word is the Rock

Now, I am going to focus in on the interpretations that came from many of the protestant reformers, but I must point out that from the very early years of the church there were different interpretations of Matthew 16:18. The reason I want to focus on the reformers is that those different earlier interpretations were not openly discussed in a public forum prior to the 1500's. The different interpretations prior to the 1500's came from biblically trained scholars, usually Catholic friars who spent most of their time writing commentaries on the meaning of scripture for other scholars to read and discuss. These commentaries were typically written in Latin and were not readily accessible to the general public. The public did not usually read at all, but when they did, it was in the vernacular, the local language of the people. It was generally acceptable to the Catholic Church for the friars to research and discuss scriptures among fellow scholars as long as the standard interpretation that the public saw was not contested. By the year 1550 there were at least four different interpretations of the exact meaning of "this rock" in Matthew 16:18, and a fifth came later. So, I am going to focus on these reformers because they are the ones who brought these interpretations out, formalized them, and spread them to the public as doctrine.

When the Protestant Reformation started in Wittenburg with the publication of Martin Luther's *95 theses* in 1517, a question was raised in the minds of the common people. Some started to take interest in what the scriptures said and to realize that the standard Catholic interpretation for some scriptures might not be correct. These other interpretations of Matthew 16:18 became public knowledge through the reformers who wrote in the vernacular, with grave consequences for the Roman Church. Martin Luther was the first protestant reformer and had much to say about this passage. Trained as an Augustinian friar, Luther interpreted the passage the same way that St. Augustine did: the "rock" is Jesus Himself. Augustine also said that Peter represents the Church[36]. In Augustine's *Tractate on the Gospel of John*, he writes:

> For petra (rock) is not derived from Peter, but Peter from petra; just as Christ is not called so from the Christian, but the Christian from Christ.
>
> For on this very account the Lord said, 'On this rock will I build my Church,' because Peter had said, 'Thou art the Christ, the Son of the living God.' On this rock, therefore, He said, which thou hast confessed, I will build my Church.
>
> For the Rock (Petra) was Christ; and on this foundation was Peter himself built.

So as a good Augustinian, Martin Luther says *Jesus is the rock*, but he does not leave it at that. In reading John 1:1-14, Luther would see that Jesus was also the Word –the actual scriptures, made flesh. John 1:1 says, "In the beginning was the Word, and the Word was with God, **and the Word was God**." And John 1:14 says, "**And the Word was made flesh, and dwelt among us**, (and we beheld his glory, the glory as of the only begotten of the Father,) full of grace and truth." Luther would come to say that Jesus is *the rock* in the form of the divine Word: the scriptures. On the rock of the scriptures, according to Luther, the church should be built. In 1523, Luther wrote *On governmental Authority* in which he says:

> [God]…desires that our faith be based simply and entirely on His divine Word alone. He says in Matt. 18 [16:18] 'On this rock I will build my church'… Hence, it is the height of folly when they command that one shall believe the Church, the fathers, and the councils, though there be no Word of God for

---

[36] St. Augustine was bishop of Hippo and lived from 354 to 430 AD

> it…for the Church commands nothing unless
> it knows for certain that it is God's Word…
> Therefore, in matters which concern the
> salvation of souls nothing but God's Word
> shall be taught and accepted.

The scriptures for Luther became a giant hatchet that he used to hack away at anything in the Church that was not directly found in the scriptures. Luther would attack many of the tradition-based elements of the Church. He called his principle *sola scriptura*, meaning "scripture only," and it would be one of the foundations of his entire doctrine.

Alister McGrath in his book, *Reformation Thought*, says Luther's doctrine placed the authority of the Popes, councils and theologians subordinate to Scripture, as "…**authority within the church does not derive from the status of the office-bearer, but from the Word of God which the office-bearer serves**" (153). More importantly for McGrath, Luther's doctrine says an ordinary pious Christian believer was "…**perfectly capable of reading Scripture and making perfect sense of what he finds within its pages**" (162). For Luther, the scriptures were not mysterious and anyone could and should read them and be able to understand them without formal training or special inspiration from God. Unfortunately for Luther, many people took his principle and ran with it. They read the Bible, and published their own private interpretations that Luther called heresy. Also, many people formed various radical groups that Luther would label *schwärmer* meaning fanatics or enthusiasts.

Once Luther was excommunicated from the Catholic Church, the battle lines were drawn and Catholics attacked Luther using his newfound hatchet. They would say that Jesus gave Peter the keys of the kingdom of heaven in Matthew 16:19, so clearly Peter is more important than the rest of the apostles. Luther began using harsh, condemning words for the Pope. In 1520 Luther published *Pagan Servitude of the Church*. In it, Luther says:

> Other Romanists are even more shameless in their deductions from the passage in Matthew 16[:19] ...They claim that here the Pope is given authority to decree laws, whereas, in that passage, Christ... was not giving authority to take the whole church into captivity and oppress it by any laws.

> But this dictator of ours takes and falsifies everything with his lies, and forcibly twists and deforms the Word of God.

> But in none of their books, teachings, or sermons, do the Romanists explain that these words of Scripture contain promises made to Christians... Rather, their only object has been to extend their own dictatorship by force and violence as far, as widely, and as deeply as possible.

Reason is the Rock

Huldrych Zwingli, a contemporary of Luther's also thought that Jesus was the "rock" of Matthew 16:18. In his book, *On The Lord's Supper*, published in 1526, he says, "For we find that Christ alone is the rock, Christ alone is the Head, Christ alone is the vine in which we are held secure. Therefore, Christ himself is the rock upon which the Church is built...." But Zwingli did not think that Jesus as the "rock" came in the form of divine Word only, rather that the "rock" of Jesus was in the form of divine mental illumination or reason combined with the Word.

Zwingli would also say that anyone can read the scriptures, but, unlike Luther, not everyone could understand. To understand a Christian must receive illumination from God. In Zwingli's, *On the Clarity and Certainty of the Word of God*, published in 1522, he says:

> When the Word of God shines on human understanding, it enlightens it in such a way that it understands and confesses the Word and knows the certainty of It...

> ...God's Word can be understood by a man without any human direction: not that this is due to man's own understanding, but to the light and Spirit of God, illuminating and inspiring the words in such a way that the light of the divine content is seen in his own light...

This illumination comes from the scriptures themselves – the rock that the church is built on – but in order to receive this illumination a person must consult the mind of God. Zwingli says:

> ...If you want to speak on any matter, or learn of it, you must first think like this: Before I say anything or listen to the teaching of man, I will first consult the Mind of the Spirit of God... Reverently ask God for his grace, that He may give you His Mind and Spirit, so that you will not lay hold of your own opinion but of His.

Notice the mental emphasis of Zwingli's doctrine. He uses the words "understand", "think", and "mind" – words that are associated with mental, not spiritual things. Zwingli effectively says that in consulting the Mind of God that God's Mind would shine His godly light onto our mind and we would see the reasoning behind the scripture in our mind.

Zwingli was trained in the Humanist school of thought and Luther was trained in Scholasticism. These two schools were often in competition with each other and approached scripture from different angles. Another Humanist, Desiderius Erasmus from Rotterdam, probably strongly influenced Zwingli as Erasmus wrote one of the most influential humanist works to circulate in Europe at that time, *The Handbook of the Militant Christian*. Erasmus spells out more clearly that the illumination from the Mind of God is reason. In it Erasmus says:

> I think it is agreed that the authority of the philosophers rests upon the fact that they state what is contained in a different manner in the Scriptures. What the philosophers term 'reason', St. Paul calls either 'the spirit' or 'the inner man' or occasionally the 'law of the mind'…
>
> God is Mind, the most pure and most simple Mind of all; therefore, He must be worshipped with a pure mind.

Thus, Zwingli and Erasmus modify Luther's *sola scriptura* principle. Luther believes that anyone can read scripture and understand it. He believes the meaning is obvious and literal. In the case where people's interpretations differed from Luther's, he chastised them harshly.

To Zwingli, the meaning of scripture is not so clear. Christians can read scripture and maybe even *think* they understand it with their own human reasoning, but to truly understand what the scripture says in depth, Christians need godly illumination to shine down on their mind. But to Zwingli the understanding must be mental, logical, and reasonable. In this way, Zwingli was trying to create a mental-spiritual approach to analyzing scripture.

Another similarity to Luther is Zwingli's condemnation of opposing viewpoints. If someone's interpretation differed from Zwingli's he would say that they were wrong, as he knew that his interpretation came directly from God and therefore his interpretation could not be wrong. He says in *On the clarity and Certainty of the Word of God*:

> I know for certain that God teaches me... I began to ask God for light and the scriptures became far clearer to me –even though I read nothing else –than if I had studied many commentators and expositors.

Faith is the Rock

Our fourth interpretation of Matthew 16:18 comes from John Calvin. Calvin is considered a second-generation reformer whose ministry was tied most closely to the city of Geneva, nineteen years after the controversy of Luther's *95 Theses*. Much of the groundwork of *sola scriptura* was already established by this time. Calvin said that the "rock" was neither Peter nor Christ, but faith. In Calvin's scenario of this passage, the readers should identify themselves with Peter, who is a weak, human vessel who later denies Christ. They should see that imitating Christ and declaring their faith in Him would transform them into a "rock." Calvin's writes in his *Commentary on a Harmony of the Evangelists Matthew, Mark, and Luke*:

> Hence it is evident how the name Peter comes to be applied ...to other believers. It is because they are founded on the faith of Christ... that God may dwell in the midst of them... For Christ, by announcing that this would be the common foundation of the whole Church, intended to associate with Peter all the godly that would ever exist in the world.

In John Calvin's *Reply to Sadoleto*, written in 1540, we see how Calvin places the scriptures that Luther holds so dear in a secondary place after inspiration from the Holy Spirit. He says:

> For seeing how dangerous it would be to boast of the Spirit without the Word, He declared that the church is indeed governed by the Holy Spirit, but in order that the government might not be vague and unstable, He annexed it to the Word…
>
> …it is no less unreasonable to boast of the Spirit without the Word than it would be absurd to bring forward the Word itself without the Spirit.

Now we can start to draw some observations. Luther holds the Word, the scriptures, as the highest authority and says that anyone can read and understand them because their meaning should be self-evident. Zwingli's belief that *reason is the rock* holds that the Word and the mental revelation of the Word are about equally important because you cannot have one without the other. People cannot interpret the scriptures on their own. Yet still, this doctrine emphasizes that the "light which shines down from the mind of God" must *make sense* to the reader, it must be logical to them. So, there is still a human, mental filter involved.

Calvin's *faith is the rock* doctrine does not hold the scriptures and inspiration of the Holy Spirit equal. He places the Holy Spirit above the Word, saying that the church is governed by the Holy Spirit and that the Word is only used to stabilize it. In fact, if it were not for the radical groups that form, we would not need the Word at all. We could be led exclusively by the Holy Spirit, like the Israelites who followed the pillar of fire in the Sinai desert. Because Calvin emphasizes faith and the Holy Spirit together, it is possible to have an understanding of the scripture that is not logical to the common man. Remember that Abraham's faith would have been considered irrational because both him and his wife were far up in age when he was promised to have a son. This is where Calvin sees the true believer.

Revelation is the Rock

Our fifth interpretation of Matthew 16:18 is that the "rock" is divine revelation. The basis of this view is a verse which precedes Matthew 16:18. In Matthew 16:17, it is written, "And Jesus answered and said unto him, *"Blessed art thou, Simon Bar-jona: for flesh and blood hath not **revealed** it unto thee, but my Father which is in heaven."* Interpreters keyed in on the word *revealed*. This word in Greek is απεκαλυψεν, which can be translated into English as *apocalypse, unveiling,* or *revealed.* I could not find a protestant reformer who held this belief,[37] but we can see right away that the roots of this idea are in Zwingli's *reason is the rock* and Calvin's *faith is the rock.* This doctrine became prominent around the time of the Pentecostal movement of the early 20th century.

Like Zwingli's and Erasmus' *reason is the rock* doctrine, people who believe that the *rock is divine revelation* believe that to truly understand scripture a person needs divine illumination, but

---

[37] Of course there *were* some protestant reformers who claimed direct spiritual revelation from God such as Thomas Münster or the Zwickau Prophets. Some have categorized these as *Revolutionary Spiritualists.* These reformers claimed to be prophets and claimed that all of their authority came from the Holy Spirit who instructed them directly through dreams and prophecy. Yet, I do not cite them because much of their doctrine was unscriptural, such as Münster calling for the Saxon Princes to kill both the Lutherans and the Catholics with the sword based on his "revelations." The Zwickau prophets were one of the group that Luther called schwärmer.

instead of the illumination coming in a mental form it comes in a purely spiritual form. For Zwingli or Erasmus, the Mind of God is reason, and therefore the illumination should make logical sense to the believer. If it does not make sense, then the person needs only to pray and study and eventually it will. For the *revelation is the rock* adherent, logic is not necessary and may never come.

Like Calvin's *faith is the rock* doctrine, people who believe that the *rock* is divine revelation believe that to receive the revelation from God they must have faith that God will give it to them. They must pray *expecting* God to respond to their prayer with an answer. Also, if the revelation is not logical or they do not understand it, but still lines up with scripture, then they must have faith in what God has revealed. Reason and logic are not required, only agreement with the Word of God.

Another doctrinal comparison is the differing emphasis between Word and Spirit. We have seen that Luther advocated Word only, Zwingli was balanced between the two, and Calvin emphasized Spirit more than Word. *Revelation is the rock* is balanced. Jesus is the Word made flesh and the Holy Spirit is the spirit that was in Jesus. God cannot be against Himself. The Spirit must be in agreement with the Word or the spirit that spoke is not from God. Likewise, scripture must agree with scripture. If a thing is revealed, it cannot only agree with one scripture and disagree with others. It must agree with all scriptures.

Furthermore, we should look to Jesus' example. Jesus was the Word made flesh and yet Jesus still had to be baptized with the Holy Spirit. Luke 3:21-22 says:

> Now when all the people were baptized, it came to pass, that **Jesus also being baptized**, and praying, the heaven was opened,
> **And the Holy Ghost descended in a bodily shape like a dove upon Him**, and a

voice came from heaven, which said, *"Thou art my beloved Son; in Thee I am well pleased."*

Think of that! The Word had to be baptized! So certainly, we must have the baptism of the Holy Spirit combined with the Word.

Problems

In summary, I have tried to cover each view equally, but if you have read my other essays then you know where I stand. I have not attacked any of the various doctrines but I can point out some problems with each view. The view of *Peter is the rock* is based mainly on similarities of the sounds of the words in certain languages, but these words do not sound similar in all languages, English being an obvious example. Likewise, St. Peter's bones may be under St. Peter's Basilica, but so are the bones of hundreds of others. In fact, some of those bones are not even Christian.[38] In addition, St. Peter's Basilica is not the seat of the Catholic Church, the Vatican is. Finally, rating the apostles in order of importance is obviously subjective, but Paul or even John would probably rate much higher than Peter in impact and significance.[39]

The view of the *Word is the rock* runs into some problems of interpretation. If the *rock of the church* is built upon scriptures that anyone can interpret easily, then why are there such diverse

---

[38] There are also bones of a chicken, a pig, and a horse in the same location that Peter is claimed to be buried. See St. Peter's Tomb, at en.wikipedia.org. There are approximately sixty-nine catacombs and thousands of tombs on up to five separate levels.

[39] Some people also point out that Peter is called Satan by Jesus in Matthew 16:23, shortly after the whole "rock" discourse takes place.

interpretations? Is the church built on a solid foundation or shifting sands? Luther's main focus was to remove tradition-based elements of the Church that he could find no scriptural basis for. But if a principle is to be universal then it must apply in all cases. This is one of the reasons you can hear many people today say, *"you can make the Bible say anything you want it to."* We have people who think they can just understand things mentally as written without the Spirit of God being involved. This has led to gross confusion and non-Biblical doctrine.

The view of *reason is the rock* also runs into some problems. In retrospect, perhaps Erasmus wouldn't have given so much weight to the philosophers if he were alive today, especially since so many philosophers today are atheists and agnostics.[40] Even many of the ones who believe in God cannot accept a God coming in the form of man. It is not logical to them. It does not stand up to reason. Yet, to Erasmus and Zwingli, God *is* reason.

Additionally, *reason is the rock* stipulates that whatever is illuminated makes sense to the human mind, maybe not right away, but eventually. This runs counter to some experiences I have had. When a parent speaks to a child, many times the parent does not explain *why*. The child cannot understand. The child is expected to obey because Dad and Mom know what is best, safest, and most beneficial for the child and the child could not understand the explanation anyway. The child is told something that they cannot understand. Likewise, perhaps God would tell us something that we could not understand.

The view of *faith is the rock* runs into the same problems because of Calvin's emphasis on the Holy Spirit being more

---

[40] Atheists do not believe that God exists. Some atheists go a little farther and say that there is no spiritual world at all, that all existence is material only.

Agnostics are *not sure* if God exists, most are looking for more physical evidence to prove or disprove the existence of God.

important than scripture. I have already pointed out some problems with this.

The view of *revelation is the rock* can also run into some problems. Special interpretations of the scripture can crop up from people who say that God spoke to them and revealed something new. Someone can be insane, led by demons, or just mistaken and think they have some new knowledge. Now it *is* possible to have something new, but it better line up with what is written in the Bible.

I hope that I have shed some light onto this passage and on how various interpretations reflect a certain viewpoint. A person's overall world-view determines their perspective of scripture and it reflects how they interpret each scripture.

five

SPIRITUAL FOOD

Part One

 ou are what you eat. Everything that you eat affects physical health, how you feel, your mental performance, and mood. Many people are obsessed with finding out what is the best food, supplement, nutrient, or vitamin to eat to lower cholesterol, live longer, and increase a particular performance measure. There are nutritionists and research biologists whose whole career is dedicated to finding out what to eat to improve the quality of life and make it last longer.

Likewise, in the spirit life: you are what you eat. Everything that passes *into* your eyes and ears is spiritual food. Every television program or movie you watch, every song you listen to, every conversation you partake in are foods for your spirit. If you constantly feed your spirit violence, lust, profanity, negativity, depravation, pornography, horror, Satanism, gore, and vulgarity, then what will be the condition of your spirit? What are the topics of your favorite movies? Do they contain vampires and demons, murder and violence? Do you watch TV shows where the main characters constantly cheat on their husbands? Do you play video games where you become a witch, a wizard, a gangster, a hitman, an assassin, or a drug dealer? [41] Even conversations at work are spiritual food. Gossip about coworkers and the criticism of other people is a constant stream of negativity that you are feeding your spirit.

Another important aspect to consider is what comes out of your own mouth. First, the words from your mouth show the condition of your spirit. People always say the "right things" when they can pause and think about what they want to say. But, the true spiritual condition displays itself under stress. Have a brush with death and what will you yell out? Maybe you are almost hit by a car. Will you cry out, *"Oh, Jesus!"* or will you cry out, *"Oh xxxx!"*

Second, what you say reinforces your notions and beliefs, thereby feeding your own spirit. A person who speaks positive is reaffirming the positive in their own spirit and thereby feeding their own spirit. Of course, this is just a principle of self-affirmation and has been taught to management professionals for decades; it is sometimes called positive visualization. But it *is* true in the spiritual sense. The words that you say, you also hear. The words you say can build up or tear down your own spirit. Do you speak words of faith or words of fear?

---

[41] This message is obviously for the people of wealthy nations such as the United States. Most people in poorer nations do not have these problems because they cannot afford a television set or a video game. They have different problems.

Separate Lives

Many people try to compartmentalize their lives and even have separate mental and spiritual states. They have work time and play time. They have time for family and time to mow the grass. They have their time for partying and pleasure and their time for religion and church and these times are segregated. Now, I understand that some people feel they cannot do religious things all the time, but understand this; when we are doing other things we are still continually feeding our spirit with what we are doing, what we are watching, and what we are listening to.

People typically feed themselves the world Monday through Thursday, with a double helping on Friday and Saturday. Sunday and only Sunday is for God. And only the first few hours of Sunday at that. But, understand that what you feed yourself ALL WEEK affects your spirit. Do you think that you can establish a good relationship with God when you sit down to pray if you just finished watching a horror movie full of demons?

Jesus is standing at the door and knocking, all you have to do is turn off the TV, put down the video game controller, get off the couch and go open the door! Stop filling your mind with distractions. People are so distracted with the loud noises of the world that they cannot hear God knocking on the spiritual door of their heart.

Let your mind and spirit be clean and clear – free from these distractions and negative input, and you can more easily reach up to the throne of Jesus. Sure, you still may need relaxation time, time to blow off steam, time for physical and mental enjoyment. But the *type* of relaxation time you choose has spiritual consequences.

I am not going to tell you what to do with your time. But think about this: should you play 10 hours of a video game in which you steal cars and rob people or go for a walk on a nature trail? Ask yourself, *"How does each thing affect my spirit?"* What about a picnic at the park, kayaking, climbing, bike riding, swimming, flying kites, golfing, sewing, hunting, and fishing? There are endless amounts of things you can do that affect your spirit in a positive manner.

Now that your mind is clean, your spirit is refreshed, there will be less distraction in your mind and spirit when you pray. Spiritual understanding of the Word of God will come more easily. God can communicate with you more readily. There will be a greater peace in your life. Remember, you are what you eat.

Hunger

When you become physically hungry, when the body needs nourishment, you get hunger pains. You feel a gnawing inside your belly. You have a longing for food because you are empty inside. If you are hungry enough, it becomes painful.

The same experience happens when we are spiritually hungry. There is an emptiness inside. Not empty in your stomach, but empty in your spirit. You have a longing for something to quench that emptiness. A longing in your spirit to satisfy your spiritual hunger. Most people satisfy this hunger through distraction. Keep busy and you won't think about the emptiness. Fill your void by keeping busy doing things, watching things, listening to things all day until, being completely exhausted, you fall asleep and do it again the next day.

I know because I have been there. I was empty once. I couldn't understand what was bothering me. I thought it was everything except what it really was. I thought I needed to change my job, change my life, move to a different state, or move to a different house. I thought if I could just change *something*, then I would be OK. But I found that none of those things mattered. None of those things would satisfy my spiritual hunger.

Many times we find that people who sin the most are the most hungry for the Lord. See, there is a hunger inside of them and they just do not know how to satisfy it. They are trying to quench a spiritual thirst with things of the world. And the world does not satisfy that thirst. So they pour more and more and more and more of the world down their throat, but it doesn't satisfy. You CANNOT satisfy a spiritual thirst by drinking in the world.

Now, there is a reason that thirst is there. God placed it. God made you this way so that you would yearn after Him and turn to Him. God makes a person spiritually hungry so he or she would cry out to Him to be fed.

We need spiritual food to satisfy a spiritual hunger. We need to eat good nourishment to maintain a healthy physical body and good nourishment to maintain a spiritual body. Feed on God's Word. Feed on God's Spirit. Get full of the Holy Spirit. You will be spiritually full and spiritually satisfied.

There is a reason that you are hungry. Stop trying to satisfy your hunger with distractions! They will not satisfy a spiritual hunger. We are feeding the wrong man! We, as Americans, feed and feed and feed the outer, physical man with earthly food, while the inner, spiritual man is starving! We need to reverse that situation. Starve the outer man and feed the inner man.

Six

CHURCH ORDER

Part One

he following essay is a collection of recommendations that *might* be used by a church to improve its service. Regardless if it is newly formed or well established, perfectly run or having problems, every church has somewhere to improve. The purpose of attending church is to fellowship with God in a group setting in order to worship God, and for the people to be instructed and fed of God. My recommendations are provided to try to help people achieve this purpose.

We want to go to church to accomplish something. There is a real experience with God to be had, why should we settle for anything less? If we are attending church and God is not there, then we are wasting our time. Are we there just to be seen by others? That is the worst vanity. If we can make our church the way God would have it then He will certainly be there.

I have had an opportunity; some would say unfortunate opportunity, to spend many years in a variety of different churches, some having problems and others being very well run. But even in well-run churches there can be areas for improvement. I have also seen both small and large churches that were run as everything from hostile dictatorships to an "anything-goes" commune. But there must be a right way, or a best way to do things. So here is my list based on what I have seen. I am only trying to help and if my recommendations don't fit your needs then that is fine also.

The Pastor Must Be Available For correction

Pastors, preachers, or priests have the hard job of teaching the church body the Word of God and bringing it forth in such a way as it can be received. Of course, there are occasions when preachers make mistakes, as they are human beings like everyone else. But a greater mistake many pastors make today is refusing correction because they get puffed up. They feel that because they have a PhD or trained at "such and such" college that no one can correct them. Some will take correction, but only from some one else who also has a PhD, as if God can only work through a person with a degree.

All pastors should accept correction if they get off the Word. If a member of the congregation comes to the pastor privately and says, *"Pastor ----, something you said last Sunday is bothering me because it appears to contradict the Bible in Romans --:--"* that pastor should accept that person, no matter who he is, what he looks like, what his education is, or where he comes from. Even if it comes from the church janitor. They should both go privately to the back room of the church or another private area and search out the scripture. If the pastor is right, then the church member gets educated. If the pastor is wrong then next Sunday he can clarify himself at the pulpit so that the flock is being fed properly.

The importance is not the pride of the pastor, but that the *true* Word of God is being preached. If a man is putting pride in front of the Word then there is a bigger problem.

Now, if I can say something stronger. The pastor is **duty bound** to preach the true Word of God and likewise, if a person in the congregation sees the pastor step away from the Word, then they are also **duty bound** to correct him. If the pastor is led by the Spirit of God, then he will not reject you. Of course, I am not saying to call him out in the middle of the service –that is completely out of line. Wait for an opportunity as the Holy Spirit leads and do it privately first, if he will not accept then go to the elders of the church.

Preparation and Expectation
Before Church Service

Many times a person goes to church and the Holy Spirit does not seem to move or it moves for certain people and not others. Now this may be what was supposed to happen, but in many cases, there are people who are left just sitting and watching because either **they did not properly prepare** before the service or there is no expectation of God moving.

First, let me tell you how I feel a person should prepare. On a day that a person is going to attend service they should look at it as if they are preparing to meet God. How would you prepare if you knew God would be there, right in the church building, looking at you? Look at how these American towns prepare when they find out that the President is going to pass through! They redecorate, paint, plant sod, and fancy up the whole place for perhaps a few hours visit from a man! Now we are talking about the King of kings and Lord of lords coming to visit. Jesus is not looking for us to paint the building. He is looking for reverent and humble hearts.

Let me tell you how I prepare. First, I take care of myself physically: washing, shaving, and dressing. I make sure all things are ready by the front door so nothing can be forgotten. Try to avoid last minute distractions.

Then, I take care of myself spiritually. I go to my quiet corner to be alone with God and pray. I ask Him to forgive me and cleanse me of my wrongs. I ask Him to remove any mental distractions, preoccupations, or blockages that would hinder me from receiving what He has planned for me at the service. I do not rush this prayer time, but leave plenty of time for it. Sometimes it is 15 minutes, sometimes more. Many times there is a short space of time before we head off to church. Do not get distracted, turn on the TV, or start doing things to lose your focus. Probably the best thing is just to head off to church early.

Once I arrive at the church parking lot, I say another short prayer, again, asking God to help me receive and contribute to the service as He leads me. Typically, if a person is prepared to meet God, with a clear mind, free of distractions and they come *expecting* God to make Himself known then the person will have an experience.

If you arrive early, and the service has not started yet, do not stand around and socialize. You can socialize all you want after the service is over. What I have seen is that people stand right in the sanctuary, right where they are expecting God to come and they gossip. Then, once the service is over, they run out the door as fast as they can. Don't be in the exit path in the parking lot either. This is not how it should be.

I recommend something along these lines. If your church has a lobby then quiet conversation can occur there, but all reverence and respect for God should be maintained in the main area of the church at all times. Remember, this is where we are going to meet God. Let God's sanctuary remain clean. Once you enter, find your seat and either pray or read your Bible or study notes until the service starts. The church should play soft church music during this time, either pre-recorded or from a musician. This helps tremendously to set the proper tone of reverence to the service.

People often complain that there are no more revivals. Revival means, "to make alive again." But every time God refills a person with His Spirit, it is a revival. You can have a revival every Sunday, or even every day if you are prepared to meet God and expecting to meet Him.

Next, a word about expectation. This ties into faith. Jesus said, *"For where two or three are gathered together in My name, there am I in the midst of them."* in Matthew 18:20. We must come to church **believing and expecting** God to be there because He has promised it. [42]

---

[42] More on expectation in the next book

Conduct of Opening of Service

The service should follow a schedule but also allow enough flexibility for the Spirit of God to move. Most churches have a song leader. This person opens the service in prayer, leads the congregation in two or more songs that he or she has chosen, calls for the offering, and perhaps leaves a space for a testimony or reading some church business announcements.

Each portion of the service has a specific purpose. The purpose of the song portion of the service is to worship God and prepare the people to receive the message. Some people even call this part of the service "the praise and worship." The Holy Spirit should come into the building and open the hearts and minds of the people. When singing we should sing strongly, in order to worship God. Meditate on the words of the songs as you sing them, the Holy Spirit will come. Acts 2:1 says, **"And when the day of Pentecost was fully come, they were all with one accord in one place."** You see, they were all with one accord. They all had the same mind, the same thoughts, and the same desires. They were not thinking about what to cook for dinner or working on the old Ford. They were all focused on Jesus, THEN the Holy Spirit came.

When the pastor comes out, it is time to hear the message. The time for tongues, singing, manifestations, and testimonies is over once the pastor comes out. If the Holy Spirit comes down on you during the praise and worship then you will be much more ready to receive what message God has for you. God will open up your mind and your spirit to the message that God wants you to hear and recieve.

The song leader is in charge of the flow of the service at the opening and therefore must keep control of what goes on here. If a person has a testimony, then they should talk to the song leader before the service, and if he feels that it fits, he will call you up for it. Testimonies should be relatively short and there should be only a few at each service. If you want to speak more about what God has done in your life, you can always tell people after the service is over.

Endless testimonies should not monopolize the beginning part of the service. I have seen people turn a short testimony into a 20 minute sermon. And of course, any testimony should be for the glory of God. I have been to services where people have stood up and told what *they* did for God. This is not a testimony. Testimonies tells what God did for you, not what you did for God.

Conduct During Service

Once the pastor comes out to speak, people should listen to the message. If young children are making too much noise then the parent should know how to quiet the child or take the child to a back room or cry room. It is nice to have speakers running to these rooms if possible.

I have seen all manner of distractions coming from adults also. You have to understand that the pastor should be under the anointing of the Holy Spirit and is trying to deliver a message to the people. If you interrupt him with speaking in tongues, moving up and down the aisles, talking to your neighbor, or making excessive noise, it can quench the Spirit. The pastor has to regroup. This is counter-productive. If the message is inspiring you greatly and you want to speak, hold it until after the pastor is done. Perhaps, your ministry is to speak in tongues. Yes, you have a gift from God and you have a ministry. But is your ministry supposed to happen simultaneously with the pastor's ministry of bringing the Word? No, each ministry has its own time and place. Not every ministry can happen at the same time.

On the opposite side of the spectrum, I have seen churches that are so quite that you can hear a pin drop. If I were to rise with a hearty "A*men*," a shout of praise, or saying "*That's right, Pastor*" the whole church would turn and stare. If you want an example of how God is praised in heaven, read the 5th chapter of *Revelation* where John "...**heard the voice of many angels ...and the number of them was ten thousand times ten thousand, and thousands of thousands; Saying with a loud voice, '*Worthy is the Lamb that was slain to receive power...*'**" So there is no need to sit there quietly, but when you make noise, let it be a joyful noise unto the Lord.[43] Saying "A*men*," or giving a shout of praise is perfectly alright.

Positions in Church

Some large churches have many different positions in the church but they all come down to a few categories. I will talk about just a few areas, as the rest just branch from these.

One thing I want to heavily stress is that in all things be led by the Holy Spirit. Only place yourself in a position that you know without a doubt that the Holy Spirit has led you into. Everyone has a job to do in the body of Christ, but we want to be doing the right job, the job God wants us to do. Pray and God will tell you what that job is. One of the big problems is that many people who are trying to serve God are in the wrong job. God prepares us for a service and many times we go and serve him in a different way – our own way. Serve Him in His way. Not to be funny but, the

---

[43] Psalm 66:1, Psalm 81:1, Psalm 95:1-1, Psalm 98:4-6, Psalm 100:1

problem with the body of Christ is it has people who are supposed to be a foot trying to be a nose.

Pastor – The pastor is in charge of the spiritual part of the service. The pastor's responsibility is to feed the Word of God to the people. Many small churches have the pastor doing everything. I have been to churches where the pastor is in the front playing a guitar and singing as the song leader, he brings the Word, he does everything. On Saturday he is fixing the roof and cleaning the toilets. He pays the bills, runs Bible studies, prayer meetings, and children's church. Everyone just watches him.

If a pastor has the opportunity to spend his full focus on bringing the Word and leave the rest to others, the quality of the message will be better because he will not be distracted with other things.

Elders/Board of Trustees – A person or a group of people who are in charge of maintaining the building, paying the bills, making decisions concerning church policy, and special collections. They are in charge of the finances of the church. If there is a board, the pastor may or may not be on this board.

Songs – Smaller churches might not have musicians, but all churches should at least have a song leader. Whether it is one person or a whole band, all should be full of the anointing of God. If the music is anointed and full of the Holy Spirit, then that will help tremendously in bringing the Spirit down on the congregation.

Deacon – The policeman of the church, the deacon is to keep order in the church during the service. The church is not a place of fun and frolic. The church is not a place to laugh and joke. We want to meet God here. Typically, deacons show new people their seats in the beginning, and keep order and reverence during the service. Deacons are most effective when they are polite and discrete but still speak with authority. Deacons usually are in charge of helping the poor or other outreach programs in churches that have such a ministry.

People who bring forth gifts – God gives different people different gifts. There should be people who have faith and pray for others, and intercessors. There may be people who speak in tongues, others who interpret, and still others who have discernment to know whether spiritual occurrences are from God. There are nine spiritual gifts.[44]

Teachers - Larger churches may have other offices such as teachers for the children. These teachers are not for baby-sitting or entertainment with fun and games. The teacher's purpose is to bring the Word to the children. Of course, they can do that in a fun way, but the teacher should not be spending church service time playing baseball games behind the chapel.

Some churches have other people who lead other specific services like Bible studies or prayer meetings. These are adult teachers. Do not do it unless God tells you this is your job and be led by the Holy Spirit in your performance of your duties.

Back room vs. Front room

We have detailed a little bit about people who would bring forth the spiritual gifts in a church. Now I want to talk about where they should happen, in the back room or the front. Some churches like to have people who speak in tongues and interpret right out in the congregation; other churches want that to happen in a back room before the service. I will explain both ways and try to

---

[44] 1st Corinthians 12:10

explain advantages and disadvantages of both so you can decide which way you want to go.

Churches where spiritual gifts happen in the back room typically handle it like this. There are a handful of people who are known to have the gifts of tongues, interpretations, and discernment. These people meet about an hour before the service and wait on the Lord. If the Spirit falls and a message is given, then the people with discernment know if it is of God. If all things line up, the message does not contradict the Word and the people with discernment agree that it is from God, then the message is written down and given to the pastor or song leader to be read during the service.

The benefit of this approach is control. There are spiritually wise people who are discerning the spoken word so that it is known that the message is from God. No errant messages are released to the congregation and, therefore, no confusion is introduced. One disadvantage of this approach is that it does not give newer people an opportunity to participate. Another disadvantage is that it gives the impression that the church does not want it. Or they only want it where it cannot be seen.

The other way is to have all the gifts happen during the regular service. When people speak out during the song service or immediately after the sermon it can be good for the congregation, especially for new churchgoers, because it improves faith. When a new person hears a thing spoken with his own ears and the thing takes place the next week, faith increases greatly. Paul said the unbeliever would know that God is in the midst of you when secret things are revealed.[45] The problem is that demons love to slip in with a message of tongues. Sometimes, it can be easy for them to slip in. If a person is trying to yield themselves to the Spirit of God and another spirit jumps in, sometimes the person is too

---

[45] See 1st Corinthians 14:25.

spiritually young to realize it. People who are young in spirit sometimes cannot tell the difference. This leads to confusion.

Purpose of the Gifts

Here is just a short note, because this is a huge subject. The purpose of these gifts of tongues, interpretation, and prophecy is not to just quote scriptures or repeat what is already in the Word. What is written in the Word is what the pastor is going to bring. The purpose of these gifts is not to repeat things that we know already. We have no need for someone to stand up and say, *"Behold, the Lord is coming!"* Everyone already knows that. The purpose of these gifts is to tell specific members of the congregation something that is not written in the Word and something that is significant for them. It is a direct message from God to the church body, a member, or a group of members in the church. This direct message from God should be something that is about to take place or something they should do.

Here is a Biblical examples of this. In Acts 21:9-14:
> And the same man had four daughters, virgins, which did prophesy.
> And as we tarried *there* many days, there came down from Judaea a certain prophet, named Agabus.
> And when he was come unto us, he took Paul's girdle, and bound his own hands and feet, and said, ***"Thus saith the Holy Ghost, So shall the Jews at Jerusalem bind the man that owneth this girdle, and shall deliver him into the hands of the Gentiles."***
> And when we heard these things, both

we, and they of that place, besought him [Paul] not to go up to Jerusalem.

Then Paul answered, "*What mean ye to weep and to break mine heart? For I am ready not to be bound only, but also to die at Jerusalem for the name of the Lord Jesus.*"

And when he would not be persuaded, we ceased, saying, "The will of the Lord be done."

Here is another example. At one service, the Holy Spirit spoke out to the entire congregation, but the message was for just one person that was called out by their exact name. That person was told not to go to a certain store that night. No one knew that she was planning to go there. Later, we found out there was a major car accident right in front of the store.

Many times, people pray for answers from God on things they do not understand. Answers to these specific questions often come from God through the gifts. Other people have been told to prepare for a certain event, maybe a visit from a certain person they would carry on a spiritual battle with.

Now, if there are no "witnesses," no people with discernment who can verify that the message is from God, then we have a great risk. Smith Wigglesworth recounts an interesting example where a family was told to sell their home immediately – but not to let anyone else know about this. Why? Because if this particular message was known in the church, it would have been discerned as false. There was much this evil spirit told these people through tongues and interpretation, and almost all of it was false and did not happen. But the result was that the people lost their home needlessly. (Wigglesworth, *Ever* 158) The Holy Ghost is not worried about being exposed. If you are told something from God, you can scream it from the housetops – it will still be true.

If you bring forth a message in tongues, interpretation, or prophecy and the message does NOT happen, what do you do? Clearly, the message was not from God. Do NOT give any more messages until that evil spirit is out of you. God does not lie.

Anointing vs. Professional

It is always nice to hear professionally trained people doing what they do best. I think it would be great to have a professionally trained pastor and musicians in every church. But having people who are full of the anointing of God is even better. If a person can allow God to work through them while they are playing their instruments the effect on the congregation will be much greater, even if they are not professionally trained.

When I initially felt the call of God, the first thing I did was sign up for every religious studies class I could get into. I was already in college, so I started on that path. After several years, I really thought I knew something. Then one day I had a life-changing experience with the Holy Spirit. I learned more in 40 minutes with the Holy Spirit than I had learned in 4 years in college. Now, I am not knocking college, because I did learn a lot, but FIRST seek the Holy Ghost and the anointing.

Deeds of the Nicolaitanes

The second chapter of *Revelation* has two instances where a people called "the Nicolaitanes" are mentioned. First, when God is talking to the church at Ephesus, He says in verse 6, *"But this*

*thou hast, that thou hatest the deeds of the Nicolaitanes,
~which I also hate."* Later, when God is speaking to the church in
Pergamos, in verse 14 to 15:

> *But I have a few things against thee,
> because thou hast there them that hold the
> doctrine of Balaam, who taught Balac to cast
> a stumbling block before the children of Israel,
> to eat things sacrificed unto idols, and to
> commit fornication.*
>
> *So hast thou also them that hold the
> doctrine of the Nicolaitanes, which thing I
> hate.*

Who are these Nicolaitanes? What is their significance?
Νικο in Greek translates *to conquer, to destroy*, or *without*
depending on whose translation that you read. Λαίτων (laitane)
refers to *the laity*. The Nicolaitanes may or may not have been a
real group of people, but regardless if they were or not, the idea is
that they are a people who put the congregation of the church, the
laity, under strict subjugation.[46] They *conquer* the laity. They have
church service *without* the laity's participation.

Remember that in this message God is speaking to the
church at Ephesus and the *church* at Pergamos. So, God is
describing a problem in the church. The Nicolaitanes were
overseers or overlords. They were people who ruled the church
with political–mindedness. I have seen this in many churches.
The pastor or his hand picked men are the only ones permitted to
participate. Everyone else is there to "watch the show."

---

[46] There is no historical record of a group of people called Nicolaitanes, so some
people think they were not a real group of people at all, but that "Nicolaitane" is
a title given to represent a type of behavior. In any case, whether or not they
were a real group of people, we can still learn from them.

Every person in the church has a job to do and should be a part of the church. Now of course not everyone can take the place of the pastor. We all receive our callings, our strength, and our abilities from God in portion and measure. Not everyone has the same spiritual ability, the same spiritual gifts, or the same calling. Ephesians 4:7 says, "But unto every one of us is given grace **according to the measure of the gift of Christ**." Each person needs to pray and find out from God *what* they are to do and to develop the gifts that they have been given to accomplish their God-given job.

Being a Minister

Every person in the church has a job to do and should be a part of the church. Another way of saying this is that *everyone is a minister* and everyone has their own ministry. So let us look at what the word *minister* means. According to the Dictionary, **To Minister** means:

> **To attend to the wants and needs of others**: *Volunteers ministered to the homeless after the flood.*

This is a position of SERVICE. Ministers, and everybody should be one, are to serve others using the special gifts that God gave each individually. In Matthew 20:25-28, Jesus tells us to serve one another and to NOT be like the Gentiles, who place themselves in authority over one another:

> But Jesus called them *unto Him*, and said, "*Ye know that the princes of the Gentiles* **exercise dominion over them**, *and they that are great exercise authority upon them.* ***But it shall not be so among you:***

> *but whosoever will be great among you, let*
> *him be your minister;*
> **And whosoever will be chief among**
> **you, let him be your servant:**
> *Even as the Son of man came not to be*
> *ministered unto, but to minister, and to give*
> *His life a ransom for many."*

I repeat, everyone is a minister and everyone has a ministry. Everyone is to serve others in their ministry. A ministry is not to be used to place someone in authority over another. A ministry is to help others, to serve others. Everyone has a gift. Find out what your gift is. Find out what your ministry is. Ask God, he will tell you. Start your training and start serving others and thereby serving God.

Five Fold Ministry

The term "five fold ministry" comes from Ephesians 4:11-12, where it states:

> And He gave some, **apostles**; and some,
> **prophets**; and some, **evangelists**; and
> some, **pastors** and **teachers**; for the
> perfecting of the saints, for the work of the
> ministry, for the edifying of the body of Christ:

The idea being that there are five distinct offices: apostles, prophets, evangelists, pastors and teachers, that God would use for the education of the Body of Christ. Of course, there are plenty of other jobs in the church, but these are the people that would bring forth the Word of God.

Now many times others have argued against this. They feel that if they have the Holy Ghost themselves, then that is good enough. They do not need to be taught of any man. They often quote 1st John 2:27:

> But the anointing which ye have received of him abideth in you, and **ye need not that any man teach you**:
>
> but as the same anointing teacheth you of all things, and is Truth, and is no lie, and even as it hath taught you, ye shall abide in Him.

So, there appears to be a contradiction. Additionally, it seems that I am getting off my subject of *church order*, but this will actually tie together my whole point.

No scripture can contradict another scripture because we know from the first chapter of *John* that Jesus is the Word made flesh and therefore, God cannot contradict God. So, *both* of these two scripture *must* be true. The correct answer is that we do not need MAN to teach us, but yet we still need to be taught by apostles, prophets, evangelists, pastors and teachers. If you don't catch what I am saying let me spell it out through an example.

Everyone is supposed to be filled with the anointing of God. A pastor prays before the service and becomes filled with the Holy Spirit. He then preaches his sermon, still filled with the Spirit. Now the Holy Spirit knows the secrets of the hearts of all the members of the congregation, so the Spirit may lead the pastor to say things he did not initially plan. The Holy Ghost may change the pastor's entire sermon. He is being led by the Spirit. He is a God-ordained, Spirit-filled, Word-living man. The congregation sees a man preaching, but the message of God is only coming *through* that man. The message is from God. The message is through the "anointing" that "teacheth you of all things."

Yes, we have no need of being taught by a man, but we have a desperate need of being taught of God. One of God's methods of teaching us is speaking through a man that God has chosen. We have NO NEED to be taught of a man that is merely teaching the lessons of man. We have NO NEED to be taught man's wisdom. Anyone can stand at the pulpit and say, "*don't steal*," and "*be good*."

If all I'm going to hear is the wisdom of man, I might as well stay home. In fact if all I'm going to hear is the wisdom of man, I don't even need to be a Christian. I can hear that anywhere. I want to hear the wisdom of God from God's chosen and anointed who yields himself to the power of God allowing God to speak through him. I want to be taught of God.

Teachers and Pastors

In our discussion of the five fold ministry, we saw that there are both teachers and pastors among others who are to bring the Word of God to the people. One note I would like to point out is that these five all bring the Word of God, but they all do it in a different manner. They are different ministries. To illustrate, let me make an example of the difference between teachers and pastors.

A teacher is quite simply a person who teaches, just like a school teacher, but instead of teaching the three R's they teach the doctrine of the Word of God. Now, a pastor can teach also. I have seen pastors who were teachers too. But, generally a pastor is like a shepherd. The pastor is someone who takes care of the flock of the church. This is the most difficult job of the five, in my opinion. They have to feed the Word to the young kids, the teenagers, the men, the women, the married, and unmarried. They have to feed the Word to those who are new converts and do not know much and those who are well established. And the pastor has to make sure all these groups are fed in the short time that he has the pulpit. If it were not for the Holy Spirit, this would be an impossible job.

One problem occurs when a person who is called to be a teacher who is doing the job of a pastor. Every service they teach the deep truths of God and speak on deep revelations. Typically, you will see the grown men in the congregation getting excited and everyone else bored out of their skulls. Only a small segment of the congregation is being fed. It is perfectly alright for a person to be called to be a teacher and a pastor, but seek to fulfill both roles. I think that anyone who is called to ministry should clearly ask God what they are to do and wait for a clear response from God. Find out which ministry you are called to, do not assume it is to be a pastor.

Early Dismissal

Many times toward the end of a service I see people glancing down at their watches. There are always a group of people who do not want to be in church, or who have their minds elsewhere. Likewise, sometimes there are people in the service whose hearts have been touched deeply by what the pastor has said. They want to repent. They want to be touched by God. They want to give their hearts to Jesus. They want to rededicate their lives to God. In many churches, this need is satisfied by an "altar call." I think this practice started among the Methodists, but in any case, it is done in many churches today, regardless of denomination.

Sometimes the pastor is torn. He can see many people who want to stay and many who want to leave. What should be done?

Here is my suggestion that I have seen work well. Let people leave who do not want to be there anyway. If you reach the end of the service and it looks like there are people who want to stay, say something like, *"We are going to dismiss the service now for those who want to leave, but if you want to stay and sing some songs, praise God, come to the altar, or be prayed for, then you are welcome to stay."*

I have seen this done many times and it has been my experience that when the complete group, the group that stays behind, wants to be with God that God shows up in a tremendous fashion. Once the people leave who have other things on their mind, you are left with a group that is in "one accord." This is a group that the Lord will honor and show His face to. Sometimes only one or two people will leave, but one person who is not in accord can be enough to quench the Spirit.

Summary

What I have written here should not be taken to condemn any church or denomination. I am only listing my observations to point out some things that might be used to help. I would only like to see people have a better experience, if possible. If we could improve our service, even only slightly, then why wouldn't we do that? If your service is conducted differently, and it works for you, then that is great. I only wanted to point out some things that I have seen, to make people aware. If anyone can improve, even a little, by a suggestion that I have made, then my goal has been achieved.

Seven

CYCLES

n nature, there are many cycles. One obvious one is the weather. There is winter, spring, summer, and fall. But on top of that cycle, there exist another cycle that you might not be aware of. There is a cycle of weather over much longer periods of time. On the Franklin Institute's website we can see a graphical display of this cycle for the city of Philadelphia.[47]

On the following page is displayed one overall graph covering the entire year's temperatures and recording this seasonal variability dating back to the 1870's. Also there is another similar graph showing the same sort of trace but only looking at the winter months.

---

[47] Franklin Institute's weather website can be found at <u>www.fi.edu/weather/ data2/index.html</u>

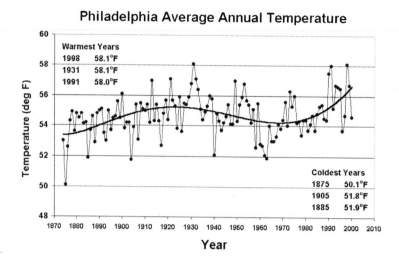

Unfortunately, older historical data is not available. I suspect that if we had data going back a greater length of time, one thousand years for example, we might see a third larger cycle.

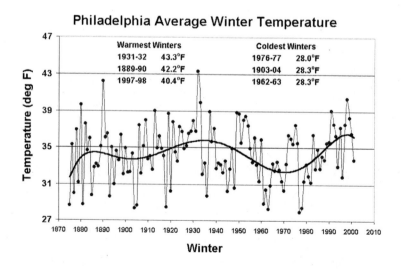

So, what we see on these graphs is that each winter does not have the same set of temperatures year after year. The temperatures over a series of years travel in a cycle.

In any case, I wanted to give a physical example as a metaphor representing what happens in the spirit world. Almost everyone knows that the physical world is a pattern of the spiritual world, that the natural is a "type" of the spiritual. In 1st Corinthians 15:46-48, Paul says:

> The spiritual did not come first, but the natural, and after that the spiritual.
> The first man was of the dust of the earth, the second man from heaven.
> As was the earthly man, so are those who are of the earth; and as is the man from heaven, so also are those who are of heaven.

So, what Paul is saying here is that we can know the pattern of spiritual things by looking at God's examples in the nature that He created. For example, we know that the three wise men looked at the stars in the sky to know the timing of spiritual events and it was a certain peculiar star that led them to Jesus.

Spiritual Cycles

Before I go on I must first state that the majority of this essay is my opinion based upon my own observations of people and history. The cycles that I outline here do not necessarily have to happen the way that I state them. I believe them to be true and correct, but your own experiences or observations may reveal differences.

Now, with that knowledge, I want to talk briefly about spiritual cycles. Everyone has cycles in their lives. A while back there was a popular theory of this phenomenon called "Biorhythms" in which it was hypothesized that a person's "ups and downs" in life were determinant on some set of biological conditions inside a person. These biological conditions could be then measured, and since we know that these ups and downs come in a cycle, a prediction could be made as to when the next upswing or downswing would come.

Of course, I think that "biorhythms" is completely phony. But, it was based on one principal that everyone can attest to, that we do have ups and downs in life, and not only in one part of life but in almost all parts. There are ups and downs in marriage life, financial life, relationships at work and with family, and also spiritual life.

Sometimes the Lord is moving you strongly in a certain direction and teaching you mightily through examples and revelation. Other time you cannot even find His face and you might feel all alone. Now this is like the small cycle of winter, spring, summer, and fall.

But there is a larger spiritual cycle that rides on top of this one. You will have ups and downs in your spirit life over short periods of time but also larger periods of time, sometimes many months together or even years. These are generally all under God's direction for the believer who is trying to follow God's leading. So, do not despair if you are in a downswing and you are trying to follow God, perhaps God is using it to show you something. Now, I am *only* talking about people who are *trying* to follow the Lord, not those who are in disobedience.

The significant piece of all this is that every peak should be at successively higher levels. So, do not worry about being in a valley. Focus on Jesus and realize that this trial will lead to a much higher peak.

cycles in Groups

Another thing many people have noticed is that these "cycles on cycles" happen to larger groups also. These cycles can be seen in families, individual churches, denominations, and the whole body of Christ. We can see the cycle affecting the whole church when we look at the history of revival movements in the 20th century.

In the late 1890's there was the well documented Welsh revival. People in Wales were not seen without their Bibles during this time and all talk was on Jesus and the daily miracles that were happening in so many homes. Many of the mainstream churches would not accept this movement, so people would gather in homes and have "cottage meetings." Much of this movement was based on intercessory prayer. People associated with this movement were Alexander Dowie, F.F. Bosworth and Gordon Lindsay.[48] But after a time there was a cooling off and many left the movement to return to the world and its ways.

In 1906, the Pentecostal revival started at the Azusa Street Mission in Los Angeles. This was a large movement and lasted for a time before it ended in organizational denominations. One of the main characteristics of this movement was speaking in tongues. The cooling off of this movement could be dated as early as 1909, but really the ripples from it lasted for decades.

---

[48] I am not listing these names to hold up any MAN but only to give you a name so that you might research later, if you feel inclined.

The evangelical crusade movement began in the 1920's. In this time, several individuals brought the Word of God to the masses in open air tent meetings. Well known evangelists of this movement were Billy Sunday, Smith Wigglesworth, Charles Price, Raymond T. Richey, Brother Freeman, and Aimee Semple McPherson. Much of their message was in support of prohibition, or a form of holiness. They also preached the Pentecostal experience that was being neglected by the Pentecostal denominations.

Another cooling came and after a time another revival movement started. It was typified by divine healing. The leaders of this movement were William Branham, Oral Roberts, and Billy Graham. This movement started around 1947. Interestingly, Wigglesworth, Freeman, and McPherson, the last three still living from the prior movement, all passed away within months of each other in 1944 and 1945. It was as if the torch had been passed. This latest revival lasted over 15 years before cooling off sometime between 1963 and 65. This movement had lasted so long that people had thought that it would never end. People were talking about the Lord's coming. There was an earnest expectation that this really was "the end" this time.

In the early 1970's the "word of faith" or "word faith" movement started. The main leader of this movement was Kenneth Hagin. The significant characteristic of this movement was the teaching of faith, speaking in faith, and speaking in authority as a son or daughter of God.[49] Hagin tried to teach faith so that those who were healed would not lose their healing because a lack of knowledge. Another cooling off followed.

---

[49] In his book, *The Believer's Authority,* Hagin said that the focus of his teaching was to bring stability to the previous revival's healings. He said that if people were going to hold onto their healing, they had to understand faith. (Hagin,xxiv)

In the early 1990's, two new movements started, but both were similar. The notable characteristic of these was divine laughter, joy, and uncontainable happiness in the spirit. People were also "slain in the Spirit" or "glued to the floor." They are mainly associated with the cities of Brownsville, Florida and Toronto, Canada. Sometimes it is called the "Toronto Blessing" or the "Brownsville Outpouring."

Once again, we have had another cooling off and many are expecting another revival on the horizon. I could say much more about this next coming revival but I will not do that here. Let us just say that as of this writing we are somewhere in the first couple stages of the next cycle.

Building cycles

Notice that each revival added something. Now that Hagin has left the scene, his message has not died. He preached faith and wrote on it extensively. When he first started, his message was revolutionary. It was right there in front of us, in the Bible the whole time, yet no one fully grasped it until God revealed it through Hagin. It was new food for everyone who heard it. Now, it is common knowledge among the believers. The Lord is restoring the body of Christ back to the hearts of the Pentecostal fathers of the first century.[50] Step by step, God is adding the missing parts back into His body to restore it back to the form it was in at Pentecost.

In the end, we see that for the believer who is pressing into the kingdom, there can be a linear progression toward perfection but that the progression will seem to go on an up and down course.

---

[50] Read Malachi 4

Each upswing should bring the follower of the message to a higher plane of understanding and a closer walk with God than the last up peak. This series of higher and higher peaks is also happening to the church as a whole.

As you pass through peaks and valleys along the way, always remember that you will be raised to a higher and higher place. Your knowledge of the nature and ways of God will be increased and you will grow closer to Him.

A Closer Look

My main goal in this book has been to provide information that is useful to an individual. But here I am writing about what happens to the church body as a whole. This is because this pattern applies to both cases. We can learn both how the Spirit is moving and how human nature reacts to the spiritual in our individual lives by looking at how the cycle moves in the whole church and vice versa.

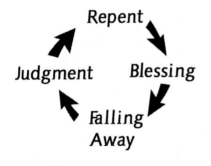

One well documented pattern is displayed to the left. First, a person repents of their sins or backsliding. Next, this penitent heart opens the door for God to come in, who then blesses both physically and spiritually. Once the person starts to receive the blessings, they become comfortable and the laziness of the flesh invariably returns. The person falls away from God by slowly decreasing their prayer time and eventually slipping back into some of their old ways, thoughts, or simply becoming lukewarm. Eventually, this leads to judgment from God.

152

Now, this is an extremely simplistic view and does not really teach us much. Of course we want to stay out of judgment, so one obvious lesson is not to backslide or fall away from our prayer life, but we can learn much more by looking at a more detailed cycle. So let us turn back to our cycle of revivals that occur to the whole church and look at those cycles with a larger magnifying glass.

In looking at the history of the Spirit of God moving through these revivals we find a more complete pattern than the one I have just shown. The cycle that I am going to present obviously does not have to happen in the order that I am presenting it, and there are many variables in every situation, so please do not be offended or misled by my generalizations. Remember, I am not trying to make statements about any one group to show their failings and errors, but am just trying to give an example that we can learn and grow from to gain a closer walk with the Lord.

This cycle that we are going to talk about has at least seven stages. Now, these stages are not any different than the simplistic four stage cycle that we just looked at, but merely is a more detailed representation of the same phenomenon.

Stage One: The Call

Initially, a person or a group of people become upset with their own sins, their own sin nature, or the sins of their community, church, country or the world. They start to pray and repent heavily. They see a need. They have a burden for the lost. They want to go deeper and deeper to something more substantial with God. They are crying out for "the rock" to be placed in the secret place of their heart. They read the scriptures and recognize that there is a gulf of difference between the relationship that the apostles had with God in the *Acts of the Apostles*, which is the relationship that we are all **supposed** to have, and the relationship that we **do** have. They want to do something about it. They want to be where God wants them to be.

The "called out" usually become disenchanted with their organization, group, church, or (denomi)nation because they do not see or seem to care about these things. The (denomi)nation lacks a prayer of repentance. It is more interested in following man's rigid established structure, dogma, chain of command, and pre-established rules than listening to the call of God.

Many times the person who feels this call is young, unaffiliated, unestablished, inexperienced, and lacking in confidence. They are all typically "unknowns." Yet, there is something special about them. They believe God's Word and are willing to yield themselves to God. They are willing to stay humble. They are willing to stay little. They are not looking to build up some great name for themselves. The Lord calls lambs not giraffes.

Stage Two: Preparation

Now the revival does not start immediately. There is usually a space of time in which God starts to prepare the person or group of people. This may be days, weeks, months, or longer. As they start to pray, repent, and seek God, they are drawn closer to Him. Daily they feel a harder and harder cry for repentance. They "sigh and cry for the abominations of the city."[51] Their prayers become longer and harder. They have a burden of prayer that grinds away the flesh. They learn how to be with God. They are being prepared for something, but they usually do not know what.

Typically, this walk with God is brought to a point where the person or group of people are totally committed to God and His Word. They will follow Him anywhere and do anything He asks. Remember John the Baptist spent years in the desert preparing before he came out to the people for a six-month ministry.

God starts to speak to them and through them. God starts to reveal to them what is the message of the hour. I feel that the depth and intensity of the coming revival is entirely dependent upon the level of preparation, prayer, and repentance of these people.

The Call
Judgment
Preparation
The Calm
Revival
Rejection and Cooling Off
Growth and Imitation

When the revival actually takes place, the masses wonder where it came from. It seems to erupt over the whole earth all of a sudden because they are not aware of all the spiritual preparation that took place. The Devil's forces will surely challenge and the saints need to be prepared.

Before the "Heart Holiness" revival in the 1750's, John Wesley was simply a college student who felt the need to gather for prayer. There was a small group of students who felt led to pray for the corruption of England. They cried out against the drunkenness and depravity. The more they cried out, the more burden they felt. The more they cried out, repented, and prayed, the more that God taught them and the more that God drew closer

---

[51] Ezekiel 9:4

to them. They received the message of holiness and sanctification. They received the message of the hour and it was burning in their hearts.

They did not receive Luther's message all over again. That message was already established and its day had already come. For them to go back would be like Moses preaching Noah's message all over again. No. This new message was revealed to them by the Holy Spirit as the message that God wanted presented for that cycle or age.

Stage Three: Revival

God's specific revelation that God wants presented for that day is given to these people to take to the masses. God revealed *justification* to Martin Luther in the early 1500's. The scriptures concerning this were always in the Bible, Luther did not make it up. But what those scriptures truly meant was not yet revealed until Luther's day. It was not yet time. Then in 1519, it was time. It was the age for this revelation. The Holy Spirit chose to reveal it to Luther and chose him to reveal it to the world. Now Luther was a nobody monk from a nobody town of Wittenburg preaching in a nobody chapel about 30 feet long and 20 feet wide with walls in decay and a pulpit made of old planks. Yet, he had the message of the hour.

Actually, if you read church history you will see that the counter-reformation[52] really started *before* Luther's reformation. Even though the Catholic reformers knew that Luther was "on to

---

[52] The counter-reformation was an effort by the Catholic Church to change for the better, to correct long-standing questionable dogma and practices. This was led by about 60 high-ranking members of the clergy who started in the "Oratory of Divine Love" between 1495 and 1517.

156

something," they still refused to acknowledge him because of who he was and where he came from. "Can anything good come out of Nazareth?" (John 1:46)

John Wesley also upset the local church clergy, who blocked him from preaching in their churches. They rejected his message from the beginning. So, he would stand in the middle of the road and preach to the people as they walked by. Many drunks and rebel-rousers hated his message because it convicted them of sin. They beat him, hit him, and threw stones at him. They did anything they could to get him to shut up! The clergy mocked him, it was unheard of to preach anywhere except in a church. One of

Wesley's solutions was to wade out into a lake near the roadways, stand waist deep in the water and keep on preaching. He would be close enough so that they could hear him but far enough away so they couldn't beat him. God gave him a message and he was going to speak it forth no matter what.

Likewise, the blessings of Pentecost were revealed to the people of the Azusa Street Mission. That building has been described as a room full of construction rubble cleared away in the center just enough to fit four benches for people to pray. They didn't even have a preacher in the beginning. People would just gather and pray, pray, pray and pray some more. Yet, the fire of God fell there like an atomic bomb. Initially, this group tried to secure the local Methodist and Baptist church buildings, but once the denominational leaders saw what these "tongues people" were doing, they kicked them out. Those ministers criticized and condemned a movement of God.

The Pentecostal ministers scrambled across the city to rent any empty building that they could find for the purpose of praying and repenting. The Azusa Street Mission is the name that most people have heard, but there were others such as the New Testament Church, the Upper Room Mission, and the Church at Eighth and Maple Streets among others. They were all empty halls or falling-down buildings. They did not hold "services" but just prayed and waited on the Lord.

In a revival, there are manifestations of the Spirit of God moving among the people. Lives are changed. The sin nature, the desire for sin, is removed from people's hearts. Illnesses disappear. Tremendous miracles happen that can be from nowhere but God. Each revival has different characteristics, but the power of God is always present in some form. And when God comes, anyone who experiences it knows without a shadow of a doubt that it is not psychology, parlor-tricks, drama, or theatrics. It is the real power of God come down among men.

People will know that the supernatural is here. People will know that God is present. The holiness group in Wesley's day described their experience as a warming of the heart. There was a tingling sensation that covered their chests.

The Shakers, today only known for their furniture, were originally a spirit filled group of believers. They were mockingly called the "shakers" because when the power of God fell on them during their revival in the 1830's and 40's, they actually shook. Their bodies trembled under the anointing of the power of God.[53]

---

[53] I do not say that the later Shaker movement and the corresponding doctrine was of God. I believe that they turned their back on God and went into fanaticism shortly after God was moving among them. But this does not discount the fact that God did move among them in the beginning. In fact, God moved in the beginning of almost every movement that ended in a denomination.

The Baptists have had a large history of revivals, between three and six depending on how you count, but the early ones were typified by ecstatic dancing in the Spirit and deep feelings of divine conviction under sin.

The revivals that occurred after 1906 all retained speaking in tongues, but also added other elements. As I said before, each revival keeps the blessings of the previous and adds something new. It is another step toward a full restoration. For example, much of the revival of the 1950's and 60's had what were critically called "holy rollers." Of course, this was initially a derogatory term, but now is a badge of honor. The name came from the practice of people bouncing and spinning in circles, hands held up and eyes tightly shut. They would spin and spin and spin under the anointing of the power of God.

The Brownsville outpouring, which started in 1995, had many similar characteristics. People would feel divine laughter, joy, and uncontainable happiness in the Spirit. People were also "slain in the Spirit" meaning that they would fall over like they were dead and just lay on the floor. Others were "glued to the floor" in that they couldn't get up. Of course this group has also been mocked with critics saying they sound like "barnyard animals." [54]

Stage Four: Growth and Imitation

Once the word gets out that God is moving somewhere among the people there will be huge crowds that flock to it. The reasons that people come are too varied to try to list, but here are a

---

[54] For your own research, the *Brownsville Outpouring* started on Father's Day, 1995 at the Brownsville Assemblies of God Church under John Kilpatrick and Steve Hill.

few. Some come for the spectacle, to mock, or to be entertained. Others are spiritualists, mediums, or occultists that flock to anything that even hints of the spiritual, whether or not it be from God. These people typically try to attach themselves to it or imitate it. Others are physically, mentally, or spiritually sick and are only coming in hopes of receiving a healing or a blessing but do not come for the associated message of the gospel. Of course there are also people who are genuine and only want to be closer to God.

When the rain falls, it falls on the wheat and the tares and both are blessed. When the rain falls, it falls on the just and the unjust and both show the results of the rain.[55] The wheat and the

tares will be present at **every single stage** of this process. Did not even Judas walk with Jesus from the very beginning?

The movement grows rapidly as people from all over flock to it, experience it, and take what they have seen back to their home town churches and try to recreate it. They bring the revival fire home with them. God vindicates the true message of the hour with signs and manifestations.

As the revival grows and spreads, there are invariably some side effects. In every movement of God, there is a twin. There is a true message and a hybrid false message. There will be people who take this new truth or experience and hybrid it to something else they already know or make up. They try to create something new or different. Many times people start doing things for personal gain or to make some name for themselves.

---

[55] Matthew 13: 24-30

The twin message can be seen dramatically in the "mind cure" movement of the 1960's. As I said before, the major characteristic of the revival at this time was divine healing. The twin emerged at the same time and it also emphasized healing but the adherents of mind cure claimed it was not from God. These spiritualists and psychologists said that the human mind had power over the body and that if a person thought or "willed" strong enough that "mind would conquer matter" and people could mentally heal themselves. Now, that divine healing has moved out of the mainstream, so has mind cure. Each new revival will have an imitation false doctrine that emerges at the same time.

Kenneth Hagin's "word of faith" message also had a twin and that twin is still present today. It is sometimes called "name it claim it" and it twists Hagin's doctrine of faith to pray for financial gain and wealth.[56]

Sometimes these imitators have the initial message or doctrine correct, but their heart or motivations are in the wrong place. Seeking after their own glory will eventually cause them to fall. This usually does much damage to the body of Christ and especially to those who were following a man instead of Jesus.

This revival is like a spiritual earthquake that shakes the whole spiritual world. It is like the ripples caused by throwing a rock into a pond. The ripples go in all different directions.

Stage Five: Rejection and Cooling Off

As the revival spreads, the imitators and the false doctrines also spread. Some people are exposed to either or both messages

---

[56] More on this in my next book.

and confusion sets it. Some people are led to extravagance and fanaticism. Because of such confusion, some people openly reject and mock it. The fanatics start teaching doctrine that is not in the Bible or contradicts it. They claim they have some "new revelation" and that "old things are passed away."

Huldrych Zwingli, a contemporary reformer of Martin Luther did this. Now, he was trying to do good for God. He led many people to the Lord, wrote extensively, and did the work of the Lord as best he could. But, he denied the virgin birth of Jesus. Something that is so clearly written in the Bible he denied.

Usually most of the fanatics either want to make a big name for themselves or to carry the revival off in some direction that they came up with in their own mind. Luther asked a group of fanatics something like, "*Have you felt the spiritual torments, that death and hell that accompanies a real true separation from the world?*" When he saw what they were really about, he rebuked them, he said, "*I slap your spirit on the snout!*" and they left.

Another group of fanatics that Luther had to deal with Were the "Enthusiasts" [Luther called them *schwärmer*] who took his justification doctrine to a ridiculous extreme. They said, "*because we are justified by faith, we not only do not have to do good works, but we can sin all we want to!*"

A small sect of Anabaptists, another group that splintered from Luther's doctrine, took over the city of Münster and tried to recreate the original apostolic church there. They called Münster the New Jerusalem and had two men claiming to be the prophets Enoch and Elijah. Unfortunately, they were not led by God, but their own vain imagination. They took up polygamy and communal living and were later wiped out.

The Brownsville and Toronto movements also had fanaticism to deal with. There are people who chase after an experience and do not care too much for the associated message. These people show up at every service expecting to be "drunk in the spirit." They try to use God to become intoxicated. The church service turns into a drug for them. They stay for the whole service and maybe even pay attention, but the real reason they are there is for that spiritual experience, to *feel* the anointing, to get drunk. They start chasing after **feelings** and trusting in things physically felt. They focus on what they feel with their flesh instead of focusing on Jesus. This makes it extremely easy for the Devil to step in.

I have seen places where people chased after fanaticism. People listen and yawn when told that Jesus died for their sins.

But tell them about someone in the congregation who has oil dripping out of his hands and they will be sitting on the edge of their seats wanting to hear all about it.

Because the fanatics, spiritualists, and extremists are leading people down a false path, a drive usually starts to formalize, codify, or organize the methods, experience, and associated doctrine. The people of the "true" movement do not want to become hybrid, so they write down what they believe. Later, they make an organization. They become formal.

"If you are to preach this new message you have to join us and do things the way we do," they say. *"We cannot have any more of this fanaticism!"* Usually, the founding members are dead, marginalized, or pushed out by now.

These organizers mean well. They are just trying to keep the Devil out, but many times they kick God out too. They determine what is expected behavior and results. They exclude anything outside of these expectations. They limit their own church experience and God to a set of man made rules. God is only allowed to move in their prescribed way. If God moves differently, then it is called "the Devil."

Funny how this is what started the whole thing, and they go right back to it. Once the new rules are established, the clergy will never deny them, even if they are later found to be wrong. They become more afraid of man than God.

I was speaking to one preacher about this and he finally said, "*Yes, I believe what you are saying is true,* [concerning the doctrine we were discussing] *but I could never preach on that because it goes against the teachings of my denomination.*"
"*Well, why don't they change their doctrine then?*" I said.
"*Oh, it's too late for that, that doctrine is well established. If we said it was wrong now, who knows what would happen?*"
"*So, you are going to deny the Word of God?*" I said.
"*No, I just won't preach on it,*" He said. "*I can't. If someone found out, I would lose my pension.*" Apparently, this group provided a pension for their preachers when they retire. Talk about not believing God to provide. I shook my head and walked away.

Another problem with the organizers is that **they place the knowledge of the revelation above the revelation itself**. Education and intellectualism about the new understanding of the doctrine becomes foremost while the actual experience of receiving the revelation is neglected. The result is a group of people who understand mentally while not having that true spiritual knowledge in the depth of their being.

The long term result is terrible. We have people who want to serve God, so they do the best thing they know how to, they go to a seminary or a Bible college. The school teaches them a tremendous amount of intellectual knowledge and they receive all the best theology available. Then, they go out to preach or to the missions. Fifty years later, you can find some that still have not had a true experience with the Holy Spirit. They can preach all day on the sacrifice Jesus made, yet they have never experienced it themselves. They have never crucified themselves with Jesus.

One last point is, of course, control. Once the power of God is unleashed to the people there comes political, social, and economic upheaval. This obviously frightens the religious and political rulers who will try to control or influence the clergy to put this thing down. *"We cannot empower the people!"* they think.

The farther these two groups, the fanatics and the organizers, move away from God, the less God is with them. The revival seems to cool off. The meetings become smaller and the Holy Spirit is not there as much and as strong. The Spirit in the Welsh revival was quenched when the old preachers pushed God out. They wanted a return to the old ways, the ecclesiastical order. They wanted to take back the control of their pulpits. Every revival is quenched when man tries to take control of it. Once Israel asked for a king too. Then there was no more need to follow the pillar of fire.

Most of the smaller revivals of the 20th century have lasted about three years. Some of the longer ones have lasted as long as fifteen years. Of course, if God would have his way, they would never end, but God is always pushed out.

Stage Six: The Calm

After this pull back of the Holy Spirit, God does not immediately judge the people. The Lord is merciful and long suffering and does not desire to judge his people. He gives us a space of time to repent. Usually, people who are spiritually minded see this and start to cry out for repentance. They see that the spiritual blessings are being removed, even though the physical ones may still be present, and they become alarmed.

If all that you look at is the physical world, then you might be wondering what these "kooks" are wailing about. All is well. We are at peace. *"Why are these people always trying to tear us down? Look how peaceful we are! Look how successful we are! Look how big our church is! We are the leading edge of the latest revival that the world has seen, so we must be in the right. God was just moving among us, and we still have the same message, we are OK, right?"* they think.

"We started from nothing and now we have a great big church with a great big budget with great big programs and a great big outreach ministry. Look at us! We are spreading across the world! Why are they crying out for us to repent?" they think.

This calm could last a few years or several decades. But if the people do not repent then there will certainly be a judgment. This is what happened in the case of the Welsh revival. The

cottage meetings started to cool off and there was a push by the clergy to return the people to their pews and the old ways. This effort of theirs was unfortunately successful. But as this revival started to cool, the Los Angeles revival started. In fact, many of the founders of the Pentecostal movement had been exposed to the experience in Wales or the revival that spread from Wales. These people had attended these "cottage meetings" and saw the power of God there. They became desperate for it in their own city of Los Angeles. They had a burning desire to recreate what was happening in Wales, so they got down on their faces and prayed for it for as long as it took until It fell. I believe their repentance stayed the move to judgment for a time.

stage seven: Judgment

Judgment appears when God fully turns his back on a people. Then the Devil steps in. All the Devil wants to do is crush, kill, and destroy. At all times he is like a wild man "looking to see who he can devour."[57] If the Devil had his way, he would destroy and kill everyone daily. Judgment can come in a variety of different ways such as natural disasters, wars, diseases, plagues, mental stress, anguish, depression, and so many others. It does not have to be something physical. It can be mental or spiritual, but the physical is obviously the most easy to see.

I am not saying that because some group turned their backs on God, that God caused a war to occur. What I am saying is that the Devil would incite the people he controls to war every single day if it were not that God was stopping him due to the prayers and faith of the true believers.

The Bible says that the political world and its rulers are controlled by Satan. Remember that Satan offered Jesus all the kingdoms of the world when he tempted Him in the desert. Satan could do this because he controls all the political powers. Luke 4:5-7 says:

> The Devil led Him [Jesus] up to a high place and showed Him in an instant all the kingdoms of the world. And he [the Devil] said to Him [Jesus], "*I will give you all their*

---

[57] 1st Peter 5:8

*authority and splendor, for it has been given
to me, and I can give it to anyone I want to.
So if you worship me, it will all be Yours."*

Satan wants to destroy you, harm you, and the ones you love. But, Satan needs permission from God to do things. Keep yourself prayed up and righteous so you will not fall into judgment. Be protected from what Satan desires to do to you. Here is an example of a form of judgment found in Judges 2:16-21:

Then the LORD raised up judges, who
saved them out of the hands of these
raiders.

Yet they would not listen to their judges
but prostituted
themselves to other gods
and worshiped them.
Unlike their fathers, they
quickly turned from the
way in which their fathers
had walked, the way of
obedience to the LORD's
commands.
Whenever the LORD
raised up a judge for them, **He was with the
judge and saved them out of the hands of
their enemies as long as the judge lived;
for the LORD had compassion on them
as they groaned** under those who
oppressed and afflicted them.
**But when the judge died, the people
returned to ways even more corrupt than
those of their fathers**, following other gods
and serving and worshiping them. They
refused to give up their evil practices and
stubborn ways.
Therefore **the LORD was very angry**
with Israel and said, "*Because this nation has*

The Call

Judgment

Preparation

The Calm

Revival

Rejection and
Cooling Off

Growth
and Imitation

violated the covenant that I laid down for
their forefathers and has not listened to Me, **I**
will no longer drive out before them
any of the nations Joshua left *when*
he died."

This is a beautiful and full illustration of the cycle and how it leads to judgment. The judge at this time was like a prophet and had the message of the hour for the people. When the judge was in the land bringing the truth to the people, the people would repent and receive revival. Then the judge would die. The people would backslide back into the world and their false gods. After a series of judges, and a series of cycles, God's long-suffering was over, His anger was full, it was time for judgment. And God's judgment was this: "*I also will not henceforth drive out any from before them of the nations which Joshua left.*"

Breaking the cycle

Now that you can see this cycle, you should have learned many things. There is a cycle of God moving in your life and using trials and tribulations to prepare you and draw you closer to Him. But there is also a cycle that we make ourselves caused by turning our backs on God.

You know that the Bible describes the relationship between God and his chosen as the relationship between a husband and wife. So, how would this relationship be if the husband had to always yell at the wife to get her to do right? Let us say that you had a wife who was an angel when you were around, but as soon as you turned your back, she was flirting with another man. How would you react if this was your wife? This is a picture of this cycle. When we turn our backs on God and go with the world, we are cheating on Him. Break the cycle.

When my wife and I are apart we call each other every night and talk about how much we love each other and how we cannot wait to be together again. How should our relationship with Jesus be? Should we chase after the world and the Devil's ways when times are good? Should we *only* cry out to God when times are bad? Break the cycle.

I gave some examples of the cycles that happen to the entire church so that we might draw out some lessons of the cycles that affect an individual. Perhaps we cannot break the cycle for the entire church but I can break the cycle for me. You can break the cycle for you too. Break the cycle.

You, as an individual, do not have to be trapped in this seemingly endless cycle of backsliding and repenting, blessings and judgment. You can be led by the Spirit of God and continually move on to better and greater things. You can be led to a closer walk with God. Break the cycle.

Eight

GOD IN A MAN

he New Testament reveals the great and wonderful story of Jesus Christ and every true Christian believes that Jesus was God in the form of a man. But, many people do not consider what this means *exactly*.

The first thing we must comprehend is that the human being is composed of a spirit, a soul, and a body. 1st Thessalonians 5:23 says:

> And the very God of peace sanctify you wholly; and *I pray God* **your whole spirit, and soul, and body** be preserved blameless unto the coming of our Lord Jesus Christ.

In Genesis 2:7, Moses also points out these three component parts:

> And the LORD God **formed man of the dust of the ground**, and breathed into his nostrils the **breath of life**; and man became **a living soul**.

He uses the words "**dust of the ground**," "**breath of life**," and "**living soul**" to signify body, spirit, and soul respectively. The breath of life clearly represents the spirit. In our above quote from 1st Thessalonians 5:23, Paul uses the Greek word πνευμα (pneuma) to mean spirit, Ψυχη (psyche) to mean soul, and σομα (soma) to mean body. Πνευμα (pneuma) is a word that is often associated with the breath (think pneumonia).

Another scripture that illustrates the difference between the spirit, soul, and body is Hebrews 4:12:

> For the Word of God *is* quick, and powerful, and sharper than any two-edged sword, piercing even to the **dividing asunder of soul and spirit**, and of the **joints and marrow**, and *is* a discerner of the **thoughts and intents** of the heart.

In Matthew 26:38, 41, Jesus speaks about this difference between spirit, soul, and body when He is in the garden of Gethsemane:

> Then saith He unto them, *"**My soul is exceeding sorrowful**, even unto death: tarry ye here, and watch with Me.*
> *Watch and pray, that ye enter not into temptation: **the spirit indeed is willing, but the flesh is weak**."*

In Luke 1:46-47, Mary makes this distinction as she is speaking to her cousin Elizabeth:

> And Mary said, "***My soul doth magnify the Lord,***
> And ***my spirit hath rejoiced*** in God my Saviour."

So, we know that the human creature is composed of these three component parts, spirit, soul, and body in every human being.

In Christianity, a person has been separated from God due to original sin. We are not physically born with a relationship with God. There is a gulf separating us from God. Our nature is corrupt, and therefore must be converted.[58] This is a part of salvation. In this process, the Spirit of God enters in and "indwells" with the believer. Thus, the Spirit of God lives in the body of the new Christian with the Christian's own spirit. Now in the case of Jesus, the Spirit in Him was wholly and completely the Spirit of God. Jesus had a physical, earthly body and that body died on the cross, but the Spirit in Him was God's Spirit in fullness. Colossians 2:9 says, "For in Him [Jesus] dwelt the **fullness of the Godhead** bodily."

So far, this is all textbook Christianity. Now let us say something interesting. There have been many men throughout the Bible who have had God *in* them performing miracles *through* them. What I am going to show is that God works through men and *in* men and that when a *man of God* is speaking forth a message *from* God it is as if God is speaking. When a man of God is performing a work of God, it is as if God is performing the work.

---

[58] There is a false doctrine called the "two souls doctrine" that states that every person's soul dies, then we receive a new one. This is false. Our soul is converted or changed, we still have the same soul, it is only changed.

God and Man

Jesus was both God and man. Remember that the human being is composed of spirit, soul, and body. Now, when a person is converted, the nature of their own spirit changes with the indwelling of the Spirit of God. This does not mean that we have two spirits or two souls as some have said. Our spirit is *converted* meaning that the old *nature* of our spirit changes and we put on a new *nature* that is given us by the Holy Spirit. The difference between all humankind and Jesus is that the spirit in Jesus was God's Spirit. Some have said that Jesus' Spirit was "God the Father."

God's full and complete Spirit was in Jesus, but the body of Jesus was a physical, earthly body. In fact, the only difference between Jesus body and any other human body was that Jesus body was virgin born. So, the human body of Jesus had all the human characteristics that we have. The Word of God says that Jesus became angry.[59] Jesus became full of compassion.[60] Jesus became hungry. Jesus became sorrowful.[61] Jesus ate food.[62] The body of Jesus was wholly and completely human.

And this was for a purpose. Redemption. The body of Jesus could die. But the Spirit inside of Him, the Spirit of God cannot die. If Jesus was ALL God then Jesus could NOT die for our sins. If the spirit, soul, AND body were wholly and completely God and not man, then Jesus could NOT die for our sins and we would still be lost. God cannot die. And yet, Jesus *was* God.

---

[59] See Mark 3:5.

[60] See Matthew 14:14.

[61] See Matthew 26:37.

[62] See Mark 14:18.

Melchisedec

Jesus was God in the body of a man. He was the full Spirit of God in a human body. In the Old Testament, there are several examples of God showing Himself veiled in human flesh. One of those is Melchisedec. In Genesis 14:18-20, it says:

> Then Melchisedec, king of Salem, brought out bread and wine. He was Priest of God Most High, and He blessed Abram, saying,
>
> *"Blessed be Abram by God Most High,*
> *Creator of heaven and earth.*
> *And blessed be God Most High,*
> *who delivered your enemies into your hand."*
> Then Abram gave him a tenth of everything.

Melchisedec was God in the form of a man. Hebrews 7:1-4 clarifies that Melchisedec is God:

> For this Melchisedec, king of Salem, priest of the most high God, who met Abraham returning from the slaughter of the kings, and blessed him;
> To whom also Abraham gave a tenth part of all; first being by interpretation King of righteousness, and after that also King of Salem, which is, King of peace;
> **Without father, without mother, without descent, having neither beginning of days, nor end of life; but made like unto the Son of God**; abideth a priest continually.
> Now consider how great this man *was*, unto whom even the patriarch Abraham gave the tenth of the spoils.

In Hebrews 5:5-6, Jesus is linked to Melchisedec, as He should be, since they are both God in the form of a man:

> So also Christ glorified not Himself to be made an high priest; but He that said unto Him, *"Thou art My Son, to day have I begotten thee."*
>
> As He saith also in another *place, "Thou art a priest for ever after the order of Melchisedec."*

We do not know where this Melchisedec came from or where He went after He left Abraham. Perhaps, God formed a body out of the dust of the earth or perhaps out of nothing and placed His own divine Spirit in that body. When the message to Abraham from Melchisedec was given, God was finished with the body, so perhaps, it ceased to exist. We do not know. But we do know according to the scriptures that Melchisedec was God in a human body and that Melchisedec did God's work and spoke God's words.

Notice that this body of Melchisedec also ate food. It was a physical body. But I believe Melchisedec could not die for our sins because his body was different than Jesus' body. Melchisedec's body was a "theophany." Theophany is simply a term that means *God made manifest*, or *God placed into a physical representation*. The difference between Jesus and Melchisedec is, of course, the blood.[63]

In order for God to take away the sin of the world He had to satisfy the penalty of death. He had to die to satisfy this penalty. Now, I say that He had to do it but really He didn't. I mean, that was God's way of doing it, but He didn't have to. We were eternally separated from Him and He did not have to save us. God

---

[63] I am sorry to just give you a hint here, but if you are interested, do a study on the difference between the terms "flesh and blood" and "flesh and bone" in the Bible.

did it out of His mercy. God did it out of His grace. God did it out of His choice.

Melchisedec could not die. The created theophany body of Melchisedec could not satisfy this requirement. Jesus had to be born in order to die. This work of God was so fantastic, so incredible, so unimaginable that even the Devil could not figure out that Jesus was God. The Devil poked and prodded at Jesus throughout His ministry trying to figure Him out. But every time the Devil questioned Him, the only response he got was, "*It is written.*" Perhaps, if we had Jesus in us, that would be the only response we would give the Devil.[64]

The Messenger of Revelation 22

Let us look at a third example in Revelation 22:6-19. This is the last chapter of the book of *Revelation* and John is looking at an "angel" who is talking and *mistakes* that "angel" for Jesus and starts worshipping him:

> And He said unto me, "*These sayings are faithful and true: and the Lord God of the holy prophets sent his angel to show unto his servants the things which must shortly be done.*
>
> *Behold, I come quickly: blessed is he that keeps the sayings of the prophecy of this book.*"

---

[64] Of course, there are other references in the Old Testament of God appearing in the form of a man. For example, Genesis 32:24-32 talks about Jacob wrestling with God in the form of a man all night long in order that he might receive a blessing.

And I, John, saw these things, and heard them. **And when I had heard and seen, I fell down to worship before the feet of the *angel* which showed me these things**.

Then said He unto me, "*See thou do it not: for I am thy fellow-servant, and of thy brethren the prophets*, and of them which keep the sayings of this book: worship God."

And He said unto me, "Seal not the sayings of the prophecy of this book: for the time is at hand.

He that is unjust, let him be unjust still: and he which is filthy, let him be filthy still: and he that is righteous, let him be righteous still: and he that is holy, let him be holy still.

And, behold, I come quickly; and my reward is with Me, to give every man according as his work shall be.

I am Alpha and Omega, the beginning and the end, the first and the last.

Blessed are they that **do His commandments**, that they may have right to the tree of life, and may enter in through the gates into the city.

For without are dogs, and sorcerers, and whoremongers, and murderers, and idolaters, and whosoever loveth and maketh a lie.

I, Jesus, have sent Mine angel to testify unto you these things in the churches.

I am the root and the offspring of David, and the bright and morning star.

And the Spirit and the bride say, Come. And let him that heareth say, Come.

And let him that is athirst come. And whosoever will, let him take the water of life freely.

For I testify unto every man that heareth the words of the prophecy of this book, If any man shall add unto these things, God shall add unto him the plagues that are written in this book:

And if any man shall take away from the words of the book of this prophecy, God shall take away his part out of the book of life, and out of the holy city, and from the things which are written in this book."

Angel in Greek is αγγελos (angelos) which can be translated both as *messenger* and *angel* and refers both to heavenly messengers (angelic beings) and earthly messengers (prophets.) The Hebrew word for *angel* is מלאד (malak), and also means "messenger."[65] The prophet Malachi took his name from this

---

[65] Additionally, αγγελos and malak are also sometimes translated as *ambassador*. The typical meaning of αγγελos is a deputy, representative, envoy, or one who is sent from God.

word. Sometimes "angel" can also be used to mean God –as in "the angel of the Lord" sometimes referring to the Holy Spirit.[66]

So, here is a prophet that is in heaven and who has the full and complete indwelling of the Holy Spirit so much that when the prophet speaks **it is Jesus speaking through him and John cannot tell the difference!** I repeat that the words are from a prophet who is in heaven and he clearly says **do not worship me - I am a man like you** - but when he opens his mouth the WORD OF GOD comes out. He says, *"I am Alpha and Omega, the beginning and the end, the first and the last"* and he says, *"I, Jesus, have sent mine angel to testify unto you these things in the churches. I am the root and the offspring of David, and the bright and morning star."* It is God speaking through a man. It is God speaking using a man's lips.

We cannot say who this prophet is because the Bible does not tell us, but I have my suspicions that I will keep to myself. But in any case, John initially thought the man was God. Why? John clearly saw him and he says his physical appearance was αγγελος. Again, αγγελος means *messenger*. So, we do not know by this description if the messenger looked like a man or an angelic being, but his physical appearance was not like God. Now, remember, this is the last chapter, and John has already seen the throne, the lamb, the lion, and the rest. He would know if it was God. So why does John make this mistake? Because it is not the physical appearance of the messenger that John is looking at.

Clearly, John is full of the Holy Spirit and it is his own spirit mingled with the Holy Spirit that witnesses to John's inner man that this is God. When you are full of the Holy Spirit, you have in you something like a spiritual detector. It is like a Geiger counter. A person full of the Spirit of God can sense other people

---

[66] Acts 8:26

who also have the Spirit of God on them or in them. But John makes the mistake because the prophet messenger has SO MUCH God in him that John CANNOT TELL THE DIFFERENCE inside of himself, in his own spirit. He cannot tell the difference between the prophet and God.

David

So far, we have looked at three examples that are getting progressively closer to home. Perhaps, you might see where I am going with this. We should have God in us just like the people in these examples. We see that the Spirit of God existed in the earthly human body of Jesus. And significantly, this was the full and complete Spirit of God in Him.

"We cannot possibly measure ourselves up to that standard! That was God!" We also have seen where God indwelt another earthly body, Melchisedec.

"We cannot possibly measure ourselves up to that standard either. That was God too!" Then, we looked at an example of a prophet with God in him.

"Well, this prophet was already in heaven! We cannot compare ourselves to this example!" But, this *is* how we are supposed to be. Every Christian should be full of the Spirit of God. The more examples I give and the closer I bring it home, the less excuses we will have for why we fall short.

Now let us look at David. We known David was king of Israel, being chosen and anointed by God. David wrote many of the Psalms and they are included in the Bible, not because David wrote them, but because they are inspired by God. Here is a portion of Psalm 22:

1 My God, my God, why hast thou forsaken me? *Why art thou so* far from helping me, *and from* the words of my roaring?

7 All they that see me, laugh me to scorn: they shoot out the lip, they shake the head, *saying,*

8 He trusted on the LORD *that* he would deliver him: let him deliver him, seeing he delighted in him.

9 But thou *art* he that took me out of the womb: thou didst make me hope *when I was* upon my mother's breasts.

10 I was cast upon thee from the womb: thou *art* my God from my mother's belly.

14 I am poured out like water, and all my bones are out of joint: my heart is like wax; it is melted in the midst of my bowels.

15 My strength is dried up like a potsherd; and my tongue cleaveth to my jaws; and thou hast brought me into the dust of death.

16 For dogs have compassed me: the assembly of the wicked have inclosed me: **they pierced my hands and my feet**.

17 I may tell all my bones: **they look *and* stare upon me**.

18 They part my garments among them, and cast lots upon my vesture.

Most of you recognize that this as one of the most quoted Old Testament scriptures that prophesied Jesus' crucifixion. But let us look at how this Psalm might have come to be.

David was probably sitting on his balcony, dwelling on the wonderful nature of the Lord, plucking on his harp when the Holy Spirit fell on him. God's Spirit so moved David that David felt the pain and despair of Jesus far off into the future. God's Spirit *inside* of David cried out, "**My God, My God, why hast thou forsaken Me?**" But, David was not forsaken sitting on that balcony. God's Spirit inside of David cried out, "**They pierced My hands and My feet.**" But, David's hands and feet were not pierced. God's Spirit inside of David cried out, "**They part My garments among them.**" But no one was there parting David's garments as he wrote the psalm. He was the king. He was surrounded by bodyguards.

God's Spirit inside of David cried out, "**I am poured out like water, and all My bones are out of joint**." But no one was doing this to David. Perhaps David's wife ran up to find out what was the matter with him. Looking at his hands and feet to see where they were pierced and finding nothing. She found David, alone, crying as he wrote the psalm.

David was so full of the Spirit of God that David cried out and spoke the WORD OF GOD. It was God speaking through David. **It was God speaking**, using David's mouth. It was God writing the psalm, using David's hand.

Paul

The Apostle Paul opens his letter to the Galatian Christians like this:

> But though we, or an angel from heaven, preach *any* other gospel unto you **than that which we have preached unto you**, let him be accursed.
> As we said before, so say I now again, If any *man* preach any other gospel unto you than that ye have received, let him be accursed...
> But I certify you, brethren, that **the gospel which was preached of me is not after**

man.

For I neither received it of man, neither was I taught *it*, but by the revelation of Jesus Christ.[67]

Now remember, Paul had been previously putting Christians to death – he was no follower of Jesus in the beginning. Now he says in this letter, "**If any *man* preach any other gospel unto you than**" the one that I, Paul, teaches, that person will be cursed by God. Paul is saying that *his* teaching is the whole and complete Truth from God. How can he say this? How can Paul claim such authority? He goes on to say that his teaching is not from man, it is from God. His teaching is not Paul's teaching, it is Jesus' teaching. Now, Paul never met Jesus physically in the flesh. In fact he only briefly met Peter and James. He says this in Galatians 1:17-19:

> **Neither went I up to Jerusalem to them which were apostles before me; but I went into Arabia, and returned again unto Damascus.**
> **Then after three years I went up to Jerusalem to see Peter, and abode with him fifteen days.**
> **But other of the apostles saw I none, save James the Lord's brother.**

So what is Paul saying here? He never met Jesus. He only met two of the apostles, and them only briefly. Yet, in effect Paul says, *"I have the whole and complete Truth from Jesus and if any person, even an angel from heaven, deviates from **what I say**, then God will curse them."* Why? Because, this is God speaking through Paul. Those letters from Paul were like God writing using Paul's hand. Paul said, "...**the gospel which was preached of me is not after man.**"

---

[67] Galatians 1:8-9, 11-12

This is the whole and complete truth from God, using Paul to communicate it to us. Never would a man, especially a man professionally trained in the law, as a Pharisee, make such a wild and audacious claim. Yet, this is what Paul does, because it is God in him doing it.

Other Examples

You will recall that when Moses came down from the mountain, His face shone like a lamp. It shone so much with the power of God that the people would not even look at him. Did Moses have a nice suntan? Is that why his face shone? No! It was God on Moses' face. The people could not stand the sight of God in the man Moses because they became convicted of their sins just looking at him. It was God in Moses that was shining, not Moses skin.[68]

Elijah the Tishbite was another man of God. He gave 400 false prophets a challenge. *"Let us both build altars to our gods and whoever's is more powerful will let fire come down from heaven,"* he said. Now, of course we know the story. Fire came down from heaven for Elijah and the false prophets were killed.[69] But was it Elijah alone who came up with this plan? No. It was God, working through Elijah. It was God in Elijah calling down fire from heaven. Only an insane man would put himself in the position of this challenge. But God placed Elijah there because it was God **in** Elijah doing the work.

Notice significantly that Elijah had no fear of the 400 or their followers and surely they all had swords. He was one man

---

[68] See Exodus 34:29-35.

[69] See 1st Kings 18:16-40.

against an army of zealots. Yet, when Jezebel said she would have Elijah killed immediately afterwards, he ran off to the wilderness like a coward. Why? Because the Spirit of God lifted off him. It was God who called fire down from heaven and God used Elijah's lips to do it. When the job was done, the Spirit of the Lord lifted off him and all that was left was Elijah the man, Elijah the coward. 1st Kings 19:1-3 says:

> Now Ahab told Jezebel everything Elijah had done and how he had killed all the prophets with the sword.
>
> So Jezebel sent a messenger to Elijah to say, "*May the gods deal with me, be it ever so severely, if by this time tomorrow I do not make your life like that of one of them.*"
>
> Elijah was afraid and ran for his life.

Do not miss that. Elijah spoke under the anointing of God and it did not rain for three years and six months. Later, he called fire down from heaven. He did this in front of crowds of people and his enemies with no fear. Then under the threat from one woman, a threat that came from a courier, not even in person, he ran for his life. He ran in fear. The Spirit had left him.

Acts 5:15-16 is a recounting of how the *shadow* of Peter would heal people. Was it Peter's shadow? Or was it God in Peter?

> Insomuch that they brought forth the sick into the streets, and laid *them* on beds and couches, that at the least the shadow of Peter passing by might overshadow some of them.
>
> There came also a multitude *out* of the cities round about unto Jerusalem, bringing sick folks, and them which were vexed with unclean spirits: and they were healed every one.

So the Old Testament prophets had God in them. And the New Testament believers had the indwelling of the Holy Spirit in addition to the filling of the Holy Spirit. But they had their own spirit inside of their bodies also.

Note that the prophets did not have the **fullness of God** in them. They only had a portion or a measure. Each had the spirit nature of God that was required for their job and *an amount* of that spirit, not the fullness. In Ephesians 4:7, it is written, "But unto every one of us is given grace **according to the measure** of the gift of Christ." Jesus had the fullness. Jesus had ALL of God in Him. Each person, whether a prophet or not, has only *a type* of the Spirit of God and only *a portion* of that type.

Thus Saith The Lord

I did a search on my computer and it produced 413 occurrences of "Thus saith the LORD" in the Bible. Now remember these words are coming out of the mouth of a prophet. These words are coming out of the mouth of a man. Yet, that MAN says, "Thus saith the LORD." You see, it is God speaking through a man's lips. Here are a few examples:

Exodus 5:1 says:
> And afterward Moses and Aaron went in, and told Pharaoh, "***Thus saith the LORD*** *God of Israel, Let my people go, that they may hold a feast unto me in the wilderness*"

Joshua 24:2 says:
> And Joshua said unto all the people, "***Thus saith the LORD*** *God of Israel, Your fathers dwelt on the other side of the flood in*

*old time, even Terah, the father of Abraham,
and the father of Nachor: and they served
other gods."*

Isaiah 37:21 says:
> Then Isaiah the son of Amoz sent unto
> Hezekiah, saying, *"**Thus saith the LORD**
> God of Israel, Whereas thou hast prayed to
> Me against Sennacherib king of Assyria:"*

So it is God speaking through these men. It is God using a man and a man's lips to deliver a message to His people. Now, remember that in the Old Testament God comes down to do a job and leaves when done.

For example, it is Isaiah the man first. God overshadows him and speaks through his mouth. In order that the people would know that it is God talking and not Isaiah, He says, *"Thus saith the LORD..."* Then after God is done, His Spirit leaves. Then it is Isaiah alone again.

God of History

Our God is often described using the term "God of history." This has two different connotations. First, it is used in comparison to other gods, such as the pagan Roman or Greek gods. These gods had mythologies surrounding them and their exploits and origins. Our God is a "God of History" meaning that we can point to actual, physical, historical events that our God took part in. These other gods did not act in history, their stories were fantasies made up by poets. They did not exist.

Now, that is a positive way to use the term "God of history," but let us look at the second way, a negative way. That is that God *only* operated in the past. God does not do things now that He did in the past. The Bible is finished being written so there is no need to have the movement of God among us. Obviously, I am in direct opposition to this line of thinking, but amazingly enough, it has been around for a long time. When Jesus tried to reveal things to the Pharisees, they responded that *they had Moses to their father.*[70] They recognized God working through a man called Moses back in history, but they could not recognize God in a man **right in front of them**. They liked having a "God of history," way far off, back in the past.

And are people so different today? I see too many people who effectively say, *we have Jesus to our father*, yet they do not recognize when God is moving right now today, **right in front of their face.**

The entire Bible from *Genesis* to *Revelation* is a history of God working through different men and women. It is a history of God working *in* different people. God performing mighty miracles, showing Himself, His truth, His promise, and His ways from inside of a man.

It is the history of the invisible God making Himself visible. It is the history of the invisible God *revealing* Himself to us using physical, natural, visible things and people. God revealing Himself in a burning bush, a cloud by day, a pillar of fire by night, and a MAN. The Old Testament is not the story of Abraham, Isaac, Jacob, Joseph and Moses, but the story of **God working through** Abraham, Isaac, Jacob, Joseph and Moses. The New Testament is not the story of John the Baptist, Jesus, Paul and Peter, but the story of **God working in** John the Baptist, Jesus,

---

[70] See John 9:29.

Paul and Peter. The book of *Acts* is not the acts of the apostles, but the acts of the **Holy Ghost IN** the apostles.

And this wonderful story **does not stop there**. Those who have studied Christian history have seen God continues to work in men throughout all history up to this very day. God was working through Iraeneus, Polycarp, St. Patrick[71], St. Martin, Martin Luther, John Calvin, John Wesley, Smith Wigglesworth, Billy Sunday, Oral Roberts, Billy Graham, F.F. Bosworth, William Branham, Kenneth Hagin and so many others. God never stopped working in people and through people.

Were these "great men of God" as so many people call them? In Luke 18:19, "**And Jesus said unto him, '***Why callest thou Me good? None is good, save one, that is, God.***'**" So, Jesus is saying that we should not even call a man *good*. Yet, these men *were* great. Why? Because it was God IN them that was great! God manifesting Himself through men.

One of the amazing things is that it is the human that is the whole problem, yet that is what God uses to solve the problem. If I could say one good thing about these human men, it is only that they sacrificed their own will for God's will.

En Morphe

The Old Testament speaks of God appearing in the form of a burning bush when He first appeared to Moses[72] and later in a cloud by day and a pillar of fire by night when the Israelites were

---

[71] St. Patrick's real name was Sucatus.

[72] See Exodus 3:2-3.

led out of Egypt.[73] Now, no Jew, Christian, or Muslim has a problem with God placing himself in these physical forms. They realize that the bush itself was not God. They realize that it was God *in* the bush. Later, God came in the form of a man in Jesus. No Christian has a problem with God placing himself in this physical form, but the Jews and Muslims reject Him.[74] Later, God appeared to Paul in a blinding light.[75] Now, I am saying that God comes in other forms. I am saying that God speaks through other people. So, who will reject it? Do we only want a "God of history" that we can read about? Or do we want a God that can speak to us, right to our face, right now, today?

Pearry Green, in his book *Acts of the Prophet*, makes this point beautifully. He says:

> In their day, the disciples found people offended because they witnessed of Jesus Christ, a man of their own generation. If their witness had been of David, people would not have been so offended. Surely there would have been no opposition had they spoken of Moses or Noah, or about any of the other prophets of old. It is no different today. If I speak of Paul, or of Peter, James, or John, or even more recently of Luther, Wesley, or Calvin, people take no offense. Even to bring to remembrance those who were known by their evil deeds, like Judas, Herod, Pontius Pilate, Pharaoh, or Satan himself brings no offense; people accept them for what they were. But to speak of a contemporary in the same manner brings out the opposition in full

---

[73] See Exodus 13:21.

[74] I believe that the Jews rejected Jesus, not because they did not believe in God coming in the form of a man, but because they did not think Jesus was *that* man. Muslims do not believe that God will come in the form of a man at all.

[75] See Acts 9:2-4.

strength, exactly as it was in the days when
the disciples witnessed of Jesus. (1)

Do Not Worship

What I am NOT saying is to worship God in these forms.
Remember the man-prophet of Revelation 22. He had God
speaking though him saying, *"I am the Alpha and Omega..."* and
yet when John tried to worship him, he said, *"Do not do it."*

Now what form is Jesus in now? Can Jesus appear in the
form of a burning bush, a pillar of fire, and a man right now
simultaneously in three different parts of the world? Of course He
can. Can God enter a man, just like He did to the Old Testament
prophets, to give YOU a message? Of course He can. Will that
man that God speaks through have a PhD? Maybe. Or he could be
a homeless person wearing filthy rags.[76] Remember, John the
Baptist wore camel hair, lived in the desert, and ate insects. Yet, he
was chosen of God to deliver a message to his chosen ones.

How Does This Affect Me?

Now, let us take that final step. What does this mean to you
and me? How does this affect me? Where should our relationship
with God be? Is this type of relationship only for the prophets and
the so-called "chosen ones"? No.

---

[76] If all the Bible characters were alive today, Moses, Paul, and Luke would
probably have had PhDs. Most of the others were common people.

God can use others to speak to you. God can use you to speak to others. And I do not mean just God telling you to talk and say what you have to say, but God speaking **through** you. Let me give you a few examples.

A few years back I was praying about a certain difficult decision I had to make and I prayed earnestly for God to tell me what to do. I fully expected God to answer me, although I had no idea how He would do it. Immediately after I finished praying the phone rang. It was an old friend from back home who I had lost touch with. I had not heard from him in over 10 years. I spoke with him and did not let on one little bit what I had been praying about. I mean why would I? Yet, he related to me a situation that he just got through and told me how he did it. Guess what? It was the exact same situation I was struggling with. He kept saying, "*I don't know what it is, but I just felt like I **had** to call you.*" Of course, I know what it was. After his phone call, I never heard from him again.

Another similar event happened to me some years ago. I didn't have much money at the time, but I had a strong feeling to take my kids to Hershey Park. It just kept coming back to me to go there, but I didn't know why. So we went. The next morning before we left to go back home, I was at the hotel playground with my children and a lonely lady on the next park bench started pouring her heart out to me. Now, I never talk to lonely ladies on park benches, but she wouldn't stop talking. After she told me all her problems, she finished off by saying, "*And I'm a Christian and I just don't know what to do!*"

Then the Spirit of the Lord fell on me. I had just gone through a similar situation and I knew exactly what to do. I knew then why I was supposed to be at that park. I said a quick mental prayer to "*Let me speak Your words, Lord*" and then I told her how I overcame through the power of God. Even though it was my mouth moving and speaking the words, I knew it was God speaking through me. That is kind of hard to explain. It is not like a possession you might see in a movie. I had complete control over my body and mouth, yet I was stepping out of the way and just letting the words flow out. I was not really thinking about what words to say. God does not put the words in your mind first, then you say them. They do not come through your mind. They just go from your spirit straight to your mouth. Your mind is hearing the words at the same time that you say them. And of course you can feel the anointing of God's Spirit on you confirming that it is Him speaking. I knew that she received it because I saw the change in her face. It was like a burden was lifted off of her. She knew God sent me there to tell her these things.

Now, these two simple examples are just a small introduction to the *many* things God can do. God can do mighty things through you, if you let Him! Do not limit God. God can speak through anyone to send a message to His people. Remember, Jesus said God would be IN us.[77] *Every* believer should have God in them. *Every* believer should have God working through them. *Every* believer should have God speaking through them. *Every* believer should yield their will to God's will so that God could use that person to fulfill and complete His work. Amen.

---

[77] John 14:16-20

Nine

BEING FILLED

everal of my previous essays may have raised questions that I would like to clear up. There is a difference between the *indwelling* of the Holy Spirit and *being filled* with the Holy Spirit. Many people do not believe there is a difference and this is a dangerous mistake.

There are huge numbers of people who have been *filled* with the Holy Spirit, many only once, and yet some have not received the *indwelling* of the Holy Spirit. They go on believing they are saved because they had an experience, they return to their worldly ways and forget about God, and now they are headed straight for Hell. This obviously concerns me. I want to see as many people saved as I can.

Misconceptions

There are two great misconceptions that I have seen. First, there is a group of people that believe that the Holy Ghost has only been available to believers since Pentecost. They think that before Pentecost, the Holy Spirit had no direct interaction with people. We will see that this is an error.

The second misconception is that being filled with the Holy Spirit was only for the old covenant **before** Pentecost and the indwelling of the Holy Spirit is for the new covenant **after** Pentecost.[78] This group believes that there are two different experiences with the Holy Spirit, but that one was for the past **and the past only** and that the other is for this present dispensation only. At least this is half correct.

I am going to show that:

1) There is a difference between the *indwelling* of the Holy Spirit and *being filled* with the Holy Spirit.

2) *Being filled* with the Holy Spirit was available to everyone since Adam up until this day, but the *indwelling* has only been available since Pentecost. So, in effect, **both different experiences with the Holy Spirit are available to believers today.**

Most Christians acknowledge that the relationship with God changed at Pentecost. I am not going to reprint the scripture quote, but read the second chapter of *Acts* if you want to know about Pentecost. Jesus told the disciples to go to Jerusalem and *"wait until..."* After a time, the Holy Ghost came down and

---

[78] Since people sometimes use the term "baptism" to mean "indwelling" and other times to mean "being filled," I will use the term "baptism" sparingly, and when used, it will mean the same thing as "indwelling."

indwelled the believers. This same Holy Ghost comes down and indwells believers up to this day.[79]

The Holy Ghost has Always Been Available

Now before Pentecost, the Holy Spirit came down on believers also, but it was a different relationship. The Holy Spirit would come down and "rest on" the person or "fill" the person, typically for a job that was to be done. Then the Holy Spirit would leave after the job was completed and the person would be spiritually alone again. Recall my example of Elijah in *God in a Man*. He had God in him while he called fire down from heaven, and yet immediately after, he ran from Jezebel because she threatened him.

It was God in Elijah calling fire down from heaven. It was Elijah, *filled* with the Holy Spirit, who called fire down from heaven. Once the Holy Spirit left, Elijah was spiritually alone. When he heard Jezebel's threats, he ran like a coward. He was a man standing alone and he was full of fear. Here are a few more examples:

In Ezekiel 2:2, the prophet says:
> ***And the Spirit entered into me** when He spake unto me, and set me upon my feet, that I heard Him that spake unto me.*

And later he says in 3:24:
> **Then the Spirit entered into me**, and set me upon my feet, and spake with me,

---

[79] For more information on the Indwelling of the Holy Spirit, read my essay *The Indwelling*

and said unto me, '*Go, shut thyself within thine house.*'

In Isaiah 61:1 the prophet says:
> **The Spirit of the Lord GOD** *is* **upon me**; because the LORD hath anointed me to preach good tidings unto the meek...

In Exodus 31:2-3, God says:
> *See, I have called by name Bezaleel the son of Uri, the son of Hur, of the tribe of Judah:*
>
> ***And I have filled him with the Spirit of God,*** *in wisdom, and in understanding, and in knowledge, and in all manner of workmanship,*

1st Samuel 19:20-24 says:
> And Saul sent messengers to take David: and when they saw the company of the prophets prophesying, and Samuel standing *as* appointed over them, **the Spirit of God was upon the messengers of Saul**, and they also prophesied.
>
> And when it was told Saul, he sent other messengers, **and they prophesied** likewise. And Saul sent messengers again the third time, **and they prophesied also**.
>
> Then went he also to Ramah, and came to a great well that *is* in Sechu: and he asked and said, "*Where are Samuel and David?*" And *one* said, "*Behold, they be at Naioth in Ramah.*"
>
> And he went thither to Naioth in Ramah: **and the Spirit of God was upon him also**, and he went on, **and prophesied**, until he came to Naioth in Ramah.
>
> **And he stripped off his clothes also,**

and prophesied before Samuel in like manner, and lay down naked all that day and all that night. Wherefore they say, *"Is Saul also among the prophets?"*

In this last example, Saul wanted David dead. God wanted David to remain alive. Saul sent his men after David. The men tried to go through an area where a large group of prophets were prophesying under **the power** of the Holy Spirit. When Saul's men tried to move through the crowd of prophets, the Holy Spirit fell on them also, stopping them dead in their tracks. Saul's men also started prophesying. Later, when Saul tried to move through, the Holy Spirit filled him so strongly that he ripped his clothes off and prophesied all night long. This was the supernatural power of God, **the anointing** of the Holy Spirit falling on these men.

2nd Peter 1:21 says:
> For the prophecy came not in old time by the will of man: but holy men of God spake *as they were moved* by the Holy Ghost.

So, this is the relationship that existed before Pentecost. The Holy Spirit came down on believers and "filled" the person for a job that was to be done. **The Holy Spirit did not** *indwell* **the believers yet.** The Holy Spirit would leave after the job was completed and the person would be spiritually alone again.

Was this relationship only for the Old Testament? No. Look at Luke 2:25-27:
> And, behold, there was a man in Jerusalem, whose name *was* Simeon; and the same man *was* just and devout, waiting for the consolation of Israel: **and the Holy Ghost was upon him.**
> And it was revealed unto him by the Holy Ghost, that he should not see death, before he had seen the Lord's Christ.

> **And he came by the Spirit into the temple**: and when the parents brought in the child Jesus, to do for Him after the custom of the law...

John the Baptist's father was filled with the Holy Spirit. Look at Luke 1:67:

> And his father Zacharias **was filled with the Holy Ghost, and prophesied,** saying...

The Promise: The Indwelling

The 11th chapter of the book of *Hebrews* is famously called the "faith chapter" because it lists many people of the Old Testament and how they had faith in God's promise, and what they did because of that faith. The stories in that chapter are often quoted for people to look up to and emulate, particularly Abraham's, yet there is one aspect that is so often missed: that all these people from the Old Testament did NOT receive the promise of the indwelling. At the end of the chapter, Hebrews 11:39-40 says:

> And these all, having obtained a good report through faith, **received not the promise**:
> God having provided some better thing for us, that they without us should not be made perfect.

Yes, all these Old Testament people were blessed and had faith, but God reserved something better for us: the indwelling, the baptism, God living inside of us. Jesus clearly said that *the promise* was the baptism of the Holy Spirit in Luke 24:49:

> *And, behold, I send **the promise** of My*

Father upon you: but tarry ye in the city of Jerusalem, until ye be endued with power from on high.

Ezekiel also prophesied of this promised indwelling in 36:27. Actually, it was God speaking through Ezekiel:

*And **I will put My spirit within you**, and cause you to walk in my statutes, and ye shall keep my judgments, and do them.*

Indwelling is a New Relationship

One of the mistakes people have made is assuming that being filled and the indwelling are the same thing, they are not. If they were the same thing then why the significant event of Pentecost? We could *already* be *filled* with the Holy Spirit before Pentecost, so Pentecost HAD to add more. In John 14:16-20, Jesus says:

*And I will pray the Father, and **He shall give you another Comforter, that He may abide with you for ever;***
*Even the Spirit of truth; whom the world cannot receive, because it seeth Him not, neither knoweth Him: but ye know Him; **for He dwelleth WITH you, and SHALL BE in you.***
I will not leave you comfortless: I will come to you.

> *Yet a little while, and the world seeth Me no more; but ye see Me: because I live, ye shall live also.*
>
> *At that day ye shall know that **I am in my Father, and ye in Me, and I in you.***

As Jesus was speaking this, the Holy Spirit dwelled **WITH** them, but later, the Holy Spirit was to dwell **IN** them, because Jesus said, ***"for He [the Holy Spirit] dwelleth WITH you, and SHALL BE in you."*** So, the relationship between the believer and God changed at Pentecost. The indwelling was this new relationship with God.

Listen to what Jesus says in John 7:37-39:
> In the last day, that great *day* of the feast, Jesus stood and cried, saying, *"If any man thirst, let him come unto Me, and drink.*
>
> *He that believeth on Me, as the scripture hath said, out of his belly shall flow rivers of living water."*
>
> **(But this spake He of the Spirit**, which they that believe on Him should receive: **for the Holy Ghost was not yet** *given*; because that Jesus was not yet glorified.)

You see, there HAD to be a difference. Here in John 7, it says the "Holy Spirit was not yet given," but we already know of accounts of people having experiences *with* the Holy Spirit. So, there must be two distinct and separate types of experiences with the Holy Spirit. There must have been a different, new type of experience with the Holy Spirit that only came *after Jesus was glorified.* Luke says above, "for the Holy Ghost was not yet *given*; **because that Jesus was not yet glorified.**"

In the writings of several of the apostles and disciples that came after the event of Pentecost we see this difference. Paul writes in 1st Corinthians 3:16-17:

> Know ye not that ye are the temple of God, and that **the Spirit of God dwelleth *in* you?**
>
> If any man defile the temple of God, him shall God destroy; for the temple of God is holy, which temple ye are.

Also, John writes the same doctrine in 1st John 2:27:

> **But the anointing which ye have received of Him abideth *in* you**, and ye need not that any man teach you: but as the same anointing teacheth you of all things, and is truth, and is no lie, and even as it hath taught you, ye shall abide in Him.

Paul says in 2nd Timothy 1:14:

> That good thing which was committed unto thee keep **by the Holy Ghost which dwelleth in us.**

Romans 8:9a says:

> But ye are not in the flesh, but in the Spirit, if **so be that the Spirit of God dwell in you...**

1 John 4:12-14 says:

> No one has seen God at any time. If we love one another, God abides in us, and His love has been perfected in us.
>
> **By this we know that we abide in Him, and He in us, because He has given us of His Spirit.**

And we have seen and testify that the Father has sent the Son *as* Savior of the world.

So, the significant event of Pentecost brought a new relationship between the believer and the Holy Spirit. Now God can actually live INSIDE the body of a man. The Holy Spirit can join with the spirit of the person.

John the Baptist

In Matthew 11:9-11, Jesus says:

> *But what went ye out for to see? A prophet? Yea, I say unto you, and more than a prophet.*
>
> *For this is he [John the Baptist], of whom it is written, "Behold, I send My messenger before Thy face, which shall prepare Thy way before Thee."*
>
> *Verily I say unto you, **Among them that are born of women there hath not risen a greater than John the Baptist: notwithstanding he that is least in the kingdom of heaven is greater than he.***

Notice that Jesus says that John the Baptist was the greatest prophet up until that time, and that the *least* in the kingdom of Heaven is greater than him. Now, some people say that the "kingdom of heaven" is a physical place where the angels and God live and therefore, this is saying that the "lowest level" angel is greater than the greatest prophet. That is incorrect.

In Luke 17:20-21, it says:

And when He was demanded of the Pharisees, when the kingdom of God should come, He [Jesus] answered them and said, *"The kingdom of God cometh not with observation:*

Neither shall they say, Lo here! or, lo there! for, behold, the kingdom of God is within you."

When WE receive the indwelling of the Holy Spirit, WE become a part of the kingdom of heaven. In fact the kingdom of God is inside of us, because God is inside of us! And the least one of us, the least one who has the indwelling of the Holy Spirit, the least one who has God in them, is greater than John. The least person who has the Holy Spirit *IN* them is greater than the greatest one who has the Holy Spirit *ON* them. The least person who has the indwelling of the Holy Spirit is greater than the greatest one who is filled with the Holy Spirit.

Free Will

Just because a person has the indwelling of the Holy Spirit does not mean that they turn into an "autonomous robot" of God. They still have their own free will and their own desires. They still have to war against the flesh. But the difference is that those who have the indwelling have God *inside* of them *guiding* them and *comforting* them.

The indwelling is like the **person** of God inside of you, in the little box of your heart, whispering to your own spirit.[80] But you do not have to obey that little voice, you still have free will. Notice that when you do not listen to this *still quite voice* you will eventually start to become miserable in you spirit. That change inside of you, the change that occurs when you receive the indwelling, will make you *want* to listen.

Eternal damnation is eternal separation from God. The misery felt in Hell is the misery caused by being eternally separated from God. When a person who has the indwelling of the Holy Spirit walks in disobedience they become separated from God. They start to feel that misery of separation in their spirit. They start to feel like Hell.[81]

You can Still Be Filled

Another mistake is thinking that people do not get filled anymore like in the Old Testament. They still do. You can be filled with the Holy Spirit whether or not you have the indwelling. You can have a filling of the Holy Spirit and *not* have the indwelling. Or you can have the indwelling and *still* have a filling of the Holy Spirit. They are two distinct experiences to be had with the Holy Spirit.

This is what motivated me to write this essay. Many people have been filled, having an experience with the Holy Spirit, and think they are done. They think they are sealed. No. The seal

---

[80] Actually, the indwelling has many, many other great qualities. This is only one of them.

[81] In my next book, there is an essay that explains this phenomenon more thoroughly.

only comes with the indwelling, not the filling. If you have only been filled, you are not sealed. Remember what Jesus said in Matthew 7:21-23:

> *Not everyone who says to Me, 'Lord, Lord,' will* **enter the kingdom of heaven,** *but only he who does the will of My Father who is in heaven.*
>
> **Many will say to Me on that day, 'Lord, Lord, did we not prophesy in Your name, and in your name drive out demons and perform many miracles?'**
>
> *Then I will tell them plainly,* **'I never knew you.** *Away from Me, you evildoers!'*

Look closer friend! The kingdom of heaven is in us. The kingdom of heaven is what we receive when we receive the indwelling of the Holy Spirit, we become a member of the kingdom. These people that Jesus is speaking of **did not enter** the kingdom of heaven. They did not receive eternal life. They did not receive the indwelling before they died. They were probably believers at one point (justified) because they were doing God's work, but they must have back-slid before they died and lost it because Jesus said that they were not to be allowed in.

Significantly, some of them *were* FILLED with the Holy Spirit **because they *did* prophecy under the anointing** power of God and they performed many miracles. So, here we have a clear New Testament example where people were filled with the Holy Spirit and were NOT allowed into heaven.[82]

---

[82] Judas is another obvious example - remember he performed miracles with the rest of the twelve when Jesus sent them out two by two. See Luke 9:1-6 or Matthew 10:5-6

Now, I am not trying to put down being filled. I highly recommend any experience with the Holy Spirit. In fact, I want everyone to be filled with the Holy Spirit. I, myself, am trying to maintain a constant filling. But, please seek the indwelling. If you had an experience with the Holy Spirit, go on with God. Seek the indwelling.

Perhaps you have been filled with the Holy Spirit. Maybe there were some external or internal signs associated with your experience. Maybe you spoke with tongues or your heart was strangely warmed. Maybe you had a strong conviction of sin or you felt like a giant weight was lifted off of your body. Perhaps you felt a nearness of the presence of the Lord. Those are all good experiences, but go on with God. Seek the indwelling.

Notice what the prophet Joel says concerning being filled with the Holy Spirit. He says that it is available to ALL flesh. It is available to everyone, saved or not, New Testament and Old, in the kingdom or not in the kingdom. God speaking through the prophet Joel 2:28 says:

> *And it shall come to pass afterward, that*
> *I will pour out My spirit **upon all flesh;***
> *and your sons and your daughters shall*
> *prophesy,*
> *your old men shall dream dreams, your*
> *young men shall see visions...*

Smith Wigglesworth preached a sermon entitled *The Baptism of the Holy Spirit* in which he said, "*Some people realize that they have had the **power** of the Lord upon them and yet have failed to receive the **fullness** of the Spirit.*" (*Holy*, 213) See, you can have an experience with the Holy Spirit and yet still not receive the indwelling. You can *feel* something, you can have the anointing on you, yet not receive the indwelling, the full person of God.

Be Filled

Paul wrote to the Ephesian Church around AD 61 during his first imprisonment in Rome. His letter is recorded as the book of *Ephesians* in the Bible. Paul had visited that church before. When Paul visited a church he stayed until it was established in the faith. He stayed for years if it was necessary. Then when he left, he would send others that were well raised in the faith, Timothy for example, to represent and answer questions and keep things straight. These churches were like his children. So with that in mind, we read Ephesians 5:18:

> And be not drunk with wine, wherein is excess; but **be filled with the Spirit;**

So, Paul is telling people of the church, people who he personally brought to salvation knowledge, to "be filled." Many of them probably already had the indwelling, yet he tells them to still "be filled." Then he tells them *how* to get filled in 19-21:

a) Speaking to yourselves in psalms and hymns and spiritual songs,
b) singing and making melody in your heart to the Lord;
c) Giving thanks always for all things unto God and the Father in the name of our Lord Jesus Christ;
d) Submitting yourselves one to another in the fear of God.

We need the indwelling, as I outlined in chapter two, but we also need to be continually **filled and refilled** with the Holy Spirit. It is fine to have the indwelling of the Holy Spirit. But seek to maintain a **constant filling** of the Holy Spirit. We need both.

The indwelling of the Holy Spirit is a one time event. Once you have the indwelling, you never lose it. Remember, you are sealed until the day of redemption.[83] The indwelling is a state of being. Once you have it, you become it. Once you experience the indwelling, you are indwelt forever. Being filled by the Holy Spirit is different. Being filled is an anointing of the Holy Spirit that comes on an individual, then leaves after a time. You can be filled with the Holy Spirit over and over again, even many times in the same day.

Now if you have been filled with the Holy Spirit just like those Old Testament prophets; you spoke with tongues once, your heart was "strangely warmed," you felt the presence of God, or you had an experience with the Lord, then that is great. In fact, I highly recommend it. But, do not stop there. Get the indwelling of the Holy Spirit. Get converted. Let your nature be changed and replaced with God's nature. We need both.

Now once you have the indwelling of the Holy Spirit, do not stop there either. Maintain a constant filling and refilling of the Spirit. We need both.

The Wind And The Fire

Notice the dramatic difference between these two manifestations of the Holy Spirit in the apostles. First, Jesus breathes on some of the apostles after His resurrection. John 20:29-22 says:

> And when He [Jesus] had so said, He shewed unto them His hands and His side.
> Then were the disciples glad, when they saw the LORD.

---

[83] Ephesians 4:30

Then said Jesus to them again, *"Peace be unto you: as my Father hath sent Me, even so send I you."*

And when He had said this, **He breathed on them**, and saith unto them, *"Receive ye the Holy Ghost"*

Now, this breath that they received was the indwelling of the Holy Spirit, but not all of the apostles were present. Notice that there was no manifestation here. There was no speaking in tongues here. It was the wind they received, not the fire. They received the breath of God, they received the *pnuema*.[84]

Later, at Pentecost, look what happens in Acts 2:2-4:

And suddenly there came a sound from heaven as of **a rushing mighty wind**, and it filled all the house where they were sitting.

And there appeared unto them **cloven tongues like as of fire**, and It sat upon each of them.

And **they were all filled with the Holy Ghost**, and began to speak with other tongues, as the Spirit gave them utterance...

At Pentecost, the disciples received both. They received everything God had to offer. They received both the wind and the fire. They received the **breath of God** (wind) and the **fire of God**. They received what the Old Testament prophets had received (fire) and something new, the wind. They received both.

In Luke 3:16, John the Baptist speaks about this new baptism:

John answered, saying unto *them* all, *"I*

---

[84] The Greek word πνευμα (*pnuema*) is sometimes translated "breath" and sometimes translated "spirit."

*indeed baptize you with water; but one mightier than I cometh, the latchet of whose shoes I am not worthy to unloose: He shall baptize you with the Holy Ghost **AND** with fire"*[85]

Notice that John says there are two separate things to happen at Pentecost: the baptism of the Holy Ghost (the indwelling, the wind, the breath, the *pneuma*) and the baptism of fire (being filled).

Nowadays, people get satisfied with only one. We need both. Some have been filled just like in the old times, but have not gone on to get more. They got the fire, but not the wind. They need the indwelling too. Others receive the indwelling and let it get cold. They have the wind with no fire. They need a refilling to get that fire back. We need both.

The Difference

The fire or being filled with the Holy Spirit has always been available to people, even back in the days of the Old Testament. We can see the types of things that happened in those people's lives due to this filling. The filling produces outward signs and manifestations of the Spirit. It produces a physical manifestation of the supernatural.

When a person is filled with the Holy Spirit there is a outward display of something supernatural. There might be

---

[85] This is also in Matthew 3:11

tongues, prophecy, divine laughter, or being slain in the spirit.[86]
Remember 2nd Peter 1:21 says:

> For the prophecy came not in old time by
> the will of man: but holy men of God spake **as
> they were moved** by the Holy Ghost.

The signs of the indwelling are generally internal.
Remember, the Holy Spirit was already available to us in the form
of a filling, yet Jesus said He was going to send us the Holy Spirit
to do two main things: to comfort us, and to teach us. In John 14,
Jesus describes the Holy Spirit as both the Comforter and the
Teacher:

> *And I will pray the Father, and **He shall
> give you another Comforter**, that He
> may abide with you for ever;*
> *Even the Spirit of Truth; whom the
> world cannot receive, because it seeth Him
> not, neither knoweth Him: but ye know
> Him; for **He dwelleth with you, and
> shall be in you.***
> *I will not leave you comfortless: I will
> come to you. (16-18)*
> *At that day ye shall know that I am in
> My Father, and ye in Me, and I in you. (20)*
> ***But the Comforter, which is the
> Holy Ghost,** whom the Father will send
> in My name, **He shall teach you all
> things,** and bring all things to your*

---

[86] Many times when a person is filled with the Holy Spirit they speak forth a
prophetic word. Here are some examples: Numbers 11:24-29, Jeremiah 1:2,
Ezekiel 1:3, Hosea 1:1-2, Jonah 1:1, Micah 1:1, Zephaniah 1:1, Luke 3:2, Luke
1:41, Luke 1:67, Acts 4:31

remembrance, whatsoever I have said unto you. (26)

The prophet Job also indicates that the indwelling of the Holy Spirit would bring teaching and understanding. Job 32:8 says:

But there is a spirit in man: and the breath of the Almighty giveth them understanding.

This new relationship with God, the indwelling, brings at least two major new things: comfort and teaching. Let me outline what several of the differences are between being filled with the Holy Spirit and the indwelling of the Holy Spirit.

The filling of the Holy Spirit is an **influence** that comes on the meeting or the church service. It is the **power** of the Spirit. It is the **anointing**. Being filled with the Holy Spirit brings forth the **manifestation** of the nine spiritual gifts, such as prophecy, tongues, and interpretations. **It produces outward physical signs.** A person is not sealed when they are filled. **Anyone can be filled with the Holy Spirit over and over again, even many times in the same day.**

The indwelling is a different experience with the Holy Spirit. It is much more than an influence, a power, or an anointing; **It is the person of God.** The indwelling brings the Holy Spirit in the form of a **teacher** and a **comforter**. It **quickens** the flesh of a person to make it **spiritually alive** and therefore spiritually aware. When a person receives the indwelling, they become as little children and their hard heart is taken away. Smith Wigglesworth described it as "a heart that is broken and melted with the love of God." [87] A person receives the seal of God when they receive the indwelling, then they can no longer lose their salvation. When a

---

[87] Wigglesworth, *The Complete*, 15

person has the indwelling, they "enter" the kingdom of God. the indwelling is a one time event. Once you get It, you have It, and you can never lose It.

conclusion

Some people who are reading this may be nervous or a bit concerned right now. You may have just been made aware of something and it has brought in an uncertainty of where you stand with God. *"I felt the Holy Spirit before, and I was sure that I got It, now I am not so sure!"* you might be thinking. Others will reject this message simply because they do not want to deal with this possibility. I hope no one does that.

It is alright to be uncertain. Evaluate your position and get certain. I believe everyone should always know where they stand with God. Everyone should be able to stand up and declare their position. *"I am justified and I am pressing on towards receiving the Holy Spirit!"* one could say.
"I am justified, sanctified, and filled with the Holy Spirit and I am pressing on to the indwelling!" another might say. It is not like a race, let God work with you individually to grow toward perfection.

If you now realize that you do not have the indwelling, go on with God and get it. Let the searching of the Holy Spirit tell you what you need to do, where your weaknesses are, and where your resistances to Him are. Work on those areas. Make an effort to get closer to God. As you step toward Him, He will step toward you.

Remember He has promised it. Do not despair. Hold onto that faith and listen to God. He **promised** in His Word that those who believe on Him **will be** saved. Hold onto that promise and pray. The Holy Spirit WILL come. He has promised it. Remember what Peter told the people of Jerusalem in Acts 2:38-39:

> Then Peter said unto them, "*Repent, and be baptized every one of you in the name of Jesus Christ for the remission of sins, **and ye SHALL receive the gift of the Holy Ghost.***
>
> *For **the promise is unto you**, and to your children, and to all that are afar off, even as many as the Lord our God shall call.*"

You *can* have the Holy Spirit, now, as a possession. You *can* have the quickening of your dead, carnal body to a new spiritual body. You *can* have the indwelling of the Holy Spirit. You *can* have eternal life, right now, inside of you. You *can* have the kingdom of God right now. You can be sealed. You can have eternal security. You can have the person of God. You can enter the kingdom of God, right now.

Ten

KNOWLEDGE AND BELIEF

 ere I would like to address the apparent contradiction between the quest for increased knowledge of God and the idea that we need faith or to only believe. I mean, I wrote this book to try to increase knowledge of God and yet, in that same book, I tell people to *only believe*. So which is it?

Parables

First let me show you that there is special knowledge to be had. It is well known that Jesus spoke in parables to large crowds and would later explain the meaning of these parables to his small select group. His disciples questioned Him as to why this was. In Matthew 13:10-11, it is written:

> And the disciples came, and said unto him, "*Why speakest Thou unto them in parables?*"
> He [Jesus] answered and said unto them, "*Because it is **given unto you to know the mysteries** of the kingdom of heaven, but to them it is not given.*"

Jesus said that there would be mysteries and that He would give the knowledge of the mysteries to His chosen. And what is the significance of obtaining this knowledge? The first chapter of *Colossians* tells us the purpose of being filled with the knowledge of God. Verse 9 says:

> For this cause we also, since the day we heard *it*, do not cease to pray for you, **and to desire that ye might be filled with the knowledge of His will in all wisdom and spiritual understanding**;

And for what **purpose**? What does this knowledge of the mysteries of God give us? Colossians 1:10-12 continues:

- That ye might walk worthy of the Lord unto all pleasing,
- being fruitful in every good work, and
- increasing in the knowledge of God;
- Strengthened with all might, according to His glorious power,
- unto all patience and long-suffering with joyfulness;
>   Giving thanks unto the Father, which hath made us meet to be partakers of the inheritance of the saints in light:

John 8:31-32 says:

> To the Jews who had believed Him, Jesus said, *"If you hold to My teaching, you are really My disciples. Then you will know the Truth, and the Truth will set you free."*

And what happens to those who do NOT obtain the knowledge about God? In Isaiah 5:13, God says:

> *Therefore My people are gone into* **captivity,** *because they have no knowledge: and their honorable men are* **famished,** *and their multitude* **dried up with thirst.**

And in Hosea 4:6, God says:

> *My people are destroyed* **for lack of knowledge:**
>
> *because thou hast rejected knowledge,* **I will also reject thee,** *that thou shalt be no priest to Me:*
>
> *seeing thou hast forgotten the law of thy God,* **I will also forget thy children.**

Only Believe

Of course, we must believe also. But believe what? Before we can believe something, we must have the knowledge of it. There are many people who make blanket statements like, *"Well, I just believe the Bible!"* or *"I just believe in God!"* And these same people have absolutely no idea what the Bible says or who God really is. I mean, the Devil believes that God *exists* and he is certainly condemned. Believing God exists doesn't get you very far. We need the knowledge and understanding of the Truth so that the Holy Spirit can quicken it to our spirit. Romans 10:13-14 says:

> For whosoever shall call upon the name of the Lord shall be saved.
> How then shall they call on Him in whom they have not believed?
> And how shall they believe in Him of whom they have not heard?
> And how shall they hear without a preacher?

Before faith can come, a person has to hear the Word. They have to accept and receive the knowledge and that knowledge, when accepted and received, will create faith. It is the revealed Word of God, rightly preached and rightly accepted that creates faith. Romans 10:17 says, "So then faith cometh by hearing, and hearing by the Word of God."

It is not the knowledge that you have that is important to God, but what you believe. But you have to be taught before you can believe. How can a person believe in a thing that they have never heard of? Knowledge comes first, then faith. But some people stop after the first step. There are many who have the knowledge of the Truth, but do not truly believe in it. There are people out there who teach faith, and yet do not practice faith. There are people out there who teach faith, but have no faith themselves.

Now, I do not want to sound like I am criticizing anyone for that, they just need to take that second step. The other day, I was watching Kenneth Hagin Jr. on television and he admitted to this same thing. He said that when he was younger, he found himself preaching his father's message of faith, and yet he saw that he did not have faith himself. I respect him for admitting to this.

So, what did he do? He stopped preaching and started praying until he got it. Then he started right back up where he left off.

First, a person gains the knowledge of some aspect of the Word, mentally. Then they have to make a choice to accept it and believe it. At this point they have a mental belief. Then, the Holy Spirit comes and through spiritual revelation binds that Truth to their spirit. Now, they "know" it spiritually. They have a spiritual knowledge and they *truly* know it. Most people stop when they only have a mental belief. They do not move on with God to obtain the spiritual belief.

Word Body

When a mystery of God is revealed it releases the Holy Spirit and quickens this divinely revealed truth to the spirit of the listener who receives it. Let me say something stronger. It is *only* the divinely revealed mystery truths of God that will turn the hearts of the people back to the days of Pentecost, back to the days of the apostolic fathers.

Now, we are not talking about mental knowledge only. Remember that Zwingli thought this way.[88] When you think the knowledge of God is mental only, you are placing a mental filter on the Word. No, when we know something, when we *truly* know something, we KNOW it deep down inside our spirit. There is no question. There is no doubt. It is a spiritual revelation, a spiritual knowledge.

Let me give you an example of this process. Maybe you are sitting in the congregation of your church and your pastor is

---

[88] If you want a further explanation on this point, See the *On This Rock* essay.

preaching on a subject. He tells you some Truth of God in such a way as you can understand It. You never heard It this way before. You accept this Truth and choose to believe It. Then the Spirit of God wells up inside of you. You can feel that anointing power of God. This is God proving to you that what is being said is the Truth and binding that Truth to your spirit. This is revelation knowledge. You KNOW this truth so much that It becomes part of you. It becomes part of your spirit. The revealed Truth of the Word becomes a part of you.

I have heard some people use the term "Word-body" to describe their inner spirit-man. They say that in the innermost spiritual part of a person is a seed, the indwelling Holy Spirit and your own spirit. 1st John 3:9 says, "**Whosoever is born of God doth not commit sin; for His seed remaineth in him: and he cannot sin, because he is born of God.**"

As we learn and grow spiritually and we receive more revelation knowledge, the Holy Spirit bonds these revealed Truths to our seed spirit. Thus as we grow in Christ, our "Word-body" grows and gets bigger. You do not have to take this description for doctrine, but I think this is can be a nice way to understand the growth of a Christian.

Gnosticism

Now, this quest for knowledge and especially the quest for special or secret knowledge can go in the wrong direction if it is not combined with the guiding of the Holy Spirit. Let me give you an example. There is a sect who claimed to be Christians in the early years of the faith, but recently has made a resurgence. They call themselves *Gnostics*, based on the Greek word γνοσις (*gnosis*) which translates to *knowledge*. They believed that there is one unknowable God and that there is a downward movement from spirit to matter. They believe that matter is a denigration of existence. Many of the myths associated with Gnosticism say that the material world was a cosmic blunder. Some other Gnostic myths have the idea of minor gods that were created by the one God. The only path to salvation, for the Gnostic, is for the divine spark in everyone to learn the "secret knowledge" that can liberate us from the world of matter. They base all of their rites on gaining or sharing secret knowledge and all their study on the knowledge of mysteries.

This same idea can be seen in the so-called "seekers." This is not a sect, but a loose title that many new-age people take. They like to study the pyramids, astrology, numerology, and the writings of mediums such as Edgar Cayce or Nostradamus. Again, attempting to *seek* some secret knowledge.

But you see that both of these are completely mental approaches and leave off faith and the guiding of the Holy Spirit entirely. They have no Spirit, no quickening. Their process is all mental. Of course both of these approaches are a false path, but I wanted to give them as examples of how people can get hung up in secrets. Paul wrote about the Gnostics in 1st Timothy 6:20-21. In this letter, Paul says:

> O Timothy, keep that which is committed
> to thy trust, avoiding profane and vain
> babblings and contradictions of what is
> falsely called knowledge [gnosis]
> -by professing it some have strayed
> concerning the faith.
> Grace be with thee. Amen.

Knowledge is a pathway to lead to faith, but again, not mental faith. The right answer is that when a mystery Truth is revealed to you, something should awaken **in your spirit**. God should be confirming to you, in your spirit, that the knowledge is

Truth. If you do not have the Spirit of God in you confirming the truth of something then all you have is a mental understanding which could be wrong. These Gnostics and "seekers" both have endless strings of esoteric knowledge that is based on fantasy. There is no spiritual awakening involved, the Holy Spirit is not present in it.

Real Truth

There *is* a real, absolute Truth. Everything is not subjective as some people say. Either two plus two equals four or it doesn't. One way or the other is true. In all things there is something that is absolutely true. God is willing to reveal the Truth to you if you are willing to look for it. And for what purpose?

Remember Colossians 1:10-12 says:
> That ye might walk worthy of the Lord unto all pleasing, being fruitful in every good work, and increasing in the knowledge of God;
> Strengthened with all might, according to his glorious power, unto all patience and long-suffering with joyfulness;
> Giving thanks unto the Father, which hath made us meet to be partakers of the inheritance of the saints in light:

And when the Truth is revealed to you, you will know it **in your spirit**. The Holy Spirit will show you what is Truth and it will increase your faith. The Truth will quicken your spirit and it will bind to your spirit so that it becomes a part of you.

The Eunuch

Now, If you are reading or studying and do not understand, then pray and God will give you understanding so that the knowledge might come to you. Remember, we have to receive the knowledge first. Sometimes we cannot even do that. But do not despair, God will help you here too. Remember Philip in Acts 8:

26 And the angel of the Lord spake unto Philip, saying, "*Arise, and go toward the south unto the way that goeth down from Jerusalem unto Gaza, which is desert.*"

27 And he arose and went: and, behold, a man of Ethiopia, an eunuch of great authority under Candace queen of the Ethiopians, who had the charge of all her treasure, and had come to Jerusalem for to worship,

29 Then the Spirit said unto Philip, "*Go near, and join thyself to this chariot.*"

30 And Philip ran thither to *him*, and heard him read the prophet Esaias [Isaiah], and said, "*Understandest thou what thou readest?*"

31 And he said, "*How can I, except some man should guide me?*" And he desired Philip that he would come up and sit with him.

35 **Then Philip opened his mouth, and began at the same scripture, and preached unto him Jesus.**

38 And he commanded the chariot to stand still: and they went down both into the water, both Philip and the eunuch; and he baptized him.

39 And when they were come up out of the water, the Spirit of the Lord caught away Philip, that the eunuch saw him no more: and he went on his way rejoicing.

If you are confused when you are reading the Word of God or when you are sitting in the church, pray to God to give you understanding. Do not give up. Pray *expecting* God to answer. God will send someone or something to you. He did it for the eunuch, He will do it for you. Remember, God does not play favorites, God is no respecter of persons.[89] James 1:5 says:

> **If any of you lack wisdom, let him ask of God, that giveth to all *men* liberally, and upbraideth not; and it shall be given him.**

Pray expecting God to answer and God will send someone or something your way that will help give you understanding. Remember Matthew 7:8 says, "**For every one that asketh receiveth; and he that seeketh findeth; and to him that knocketh it shall be opened.**" God is not the author of confusion. When you receive this knowledge, it will help create faith. The Holy Ghost will bind that new knowledge and new faith to your spirit and It will become a part of you.

Preached Jesus

A second point concerning the story of the eunuch is that Philip "**preached unto him Jesus.**" The Eunuch did not understand **anything**. The eunuch did not even understand the very first thing he needed to know. So that is where Philip started, at the first thing the eunuch needed to know. The eunuch had not yet been justified. He did not yet receive the Spirit of Christ. So, he could not understand anything deeper. Philip did not try to preach prosperity, glorification, or even the indwelling. Philip started out with Jesus.

---

[89] See Romans 2:11, Ephesians 6:9, or Colossians 3:25, Deuteronomy 10:17.

I find that many people try to understand things that they are not ready for, then they become frustrated, they misinterpret and introduce errors. First, seek the Spirit of Christ and the kingdom of God, then you will be able to understand deeper things.

It is my opinion that without the Holy Spirit, a person cannot even understand half of the spiritual material found in the Bible.

First, receive the Spirit of Christ, get the saving knowledge of Jesus Christ and become justified. Next, seek after the baptism of the Holy Spirit. Find out everything you need to know to get It. Fix your eyes on that goal. In Luke 17:20-21, it says:

> And when He [Jesus] was demanded of the Pharisees, when the kingdom of God should come, He [Jesus] answered them and said, *"The kingdom of God cometh not with observation:*
>
> *Neither shall they say, Lo here! or, lo there! for, behold,* **the kingdom of God is within you."**

We know that the kingdom of God is in us **if we have the indwelling of the Holy Spirit** and Jesus said *"seek ye first the kingdom of God"* in both Matthew 6:33 and Luke 12:31. So, we would do well to obey Him. Once you have received the indwelling, you can more easily receive revelation on many other topics.

If you are not justified seek that first. Seek the knowledge to become justified. Once you are justified, seek the kingdom of God, seek the indwelling. Once you have the indwelling, follow the leading of the Lord and much will open up to you.

Eleven

INIQUITY

n this essay, I am trying to explain how one aspect of sanctification takes place. I am trying to explain how the inner desires for sin can start and how they can be removed. The process of sanctification is somewhat independent of where you stand as far as justification, being filled with the Holy Spirit, or having the indwelling. Sanctification is a process, not a state of being. This process continues throughout our lives. God is always trying to pull us toward perfection, regardless of how much we have progressed.

I am going to prove that:

1)   Some people have a "curse-nature" upon them based on what their parents or grandparents have done

2)   We can be free from any generational curse or "curse-nature" that has been placed on us

What is a nature?

Here are dictionary definitions of *nature* and *spirit*:

Nature: **The inherent character of a person, An inner force in an individual. A behavior.**

Spirit: **The activating principle influencing a person, A special attitude or frame of mind**: *the money-making spirit was for a time driven back.*

I say that the nature of a person is the behavior of the spirit of the person. That is to say that the spirit inside of a person is what drives the behavior or the outside actions. The unseen invisible spirit of a person causes the seen or the nature of the person. The two are different but tied so close together because one is the thing itself and one is the action of the thing.

For example, we can say that a person who is born in the United States and acts in a patriotic fashion has an *American spirit* or *a spirit of American patriotism* or has the *nature of an American*. Many times we know exactly where a person comes from based solely on their mannerisms, the type of walk or strut they have, or the way that they move their hands when they talk.

Other examples can be found in our American high schools. In high school there are many social groups. We have jocks, nerds, homies, and goths among others.[90] Perhaps some people are only in these groups as a way to fit in and perhaps they have their own personality, but stay in one group long enough and the new person adopts the nature of the group. Their own nature changes. They become a part of the group. They start to act like one another and emulate each other. Many of these changes are so subtle that the person who is changing does not even notice it themselves. The jock has the *jock spirit* and the *nature of a jock*, for example.

Human Nature in Families

But we still think that we are individuals, right? Almost everyone has a different nature, right? Everyone thinks just a little different it seems. But upon closer observation we can find some people that have almost the same nature, behavior, or way of looking at things. They yearn after the same things and think alike. This can be especially evident in families. As the old sayings go, "The apple does not fall far from the tree" and "Like father, like son."

These sayings capture something that we all observe: that many children act just like their parents or other family members. Immediately we think that this is due to upbringing. Of course, upbringing has an influence, but almost all of us can think of a person who grew up to be just like a family member who did not

---

[90] At least that is what I hear the kids call each other

live in the house. A child who is *just like* his uncle, father, or grandfather, *who he never met.* How can this be?

Let me give you one example. I have a friend that was raised by his mother. She tells me that her *"bum husband abandoned her"* when the child was only a few months old. The father was never seen again. He was a heavy gambler and a glutton. Of course, the mother raised her son as best she could and did not expose him to any of these vices, yet he turned out just like the father he never met. Even to the point of mannerisms, ways of talking, smiling and joking. Yet, he never once met the man. How can this be?

First, I want to point out that our nature is dependent on more than just biological factors, genetics, and upbringing. We have a spirit and part, if not all, of our nature is based upon our spirit. So how is it that this "spirit nature" is passed down from generation to generation in families, even among family members that have never met?

In Exodus 20:5, it is written:

> *Thou shalt not bow down thyself to them, nor serve them: for I the LORD thy God am a jealous God, **visiting the iniquity of the fathers upon the children** unto the third and fourth generation of them that hate Me;*

And in Exodus 34:7, it is written:

> *Keeping mercy for thousands, forgiving iniquity and transgression and sin, and that will by no means clear the guilty; **visiting the iniquity of the fathers upon the***

children, *and upon the children's children,*
unto the third and to the fourth generation.

Here is another translation of that same passage:
Showing grace to the thousandth
generation, forgiving offenses, crimes and sins;
yet not exonerating the guilty, but **causing**
the negative effects of the parents'
offenses to be experienced by their
children and grandchildren, *and even*
by the third and fourth generations. (Stern's
Complete Jewish Bible)

So, according to the Bible, if a member of a family is bad, God will *visit* this iniquity onto the children in that family. Additionally, if a person is good, God will *visit* this onto the children in that family. So what is iniquity? And how do we become free from it? I mean, just because Uncle Tony was a drunkard, does little Timmy have to become one too?

Iniquity

Iniquity is a difficult term to define. The etymology of the word says it means *uneven* or *unequal*. The dictionary says it means "*absence of moral or spiritual values.*" So, most people have taken this to mean "*sin.*" And in a way it is. But the Bible clearly uses both of the words *iniquity* and *sin* in addition to the word *transgression*, so there must be different shades of meaning.

Iniquity is a **sin nature**. This sin nature causes people to *desire* to sin. These people are born *leaning* toward a certain type of sin. It is placed on the children of a sinner as a curse because the sinner did not repent when God called for repentance.[91] If they are children of gamblers, they might be born with a desire for gambling. This predisposition toward the sin is a curse. I know this sounds harsh, but it is clearly true as you can see in the Bible quotes just listed.

Freedom from Iniquity

Thank God, we can be free from iniquity just as much as any other sin. In Isaiah 53:5, several characteristics of Jesus mission are described:

> But He was wounded for our transgressions, **He was bruised for our iniquities**: the chastisement of our peace was upon Him; and with His stripes we are healed.

An interesting point about this passage is that the external wounds were for physical healing from sickness and diseases because "**with His stripes we are healed.**" And the internal injuries were for freedom from iniquity because "**He was bruised for our iniquities.**" See, the iniquity is an internal sin nature. The Lord Jesus was bruised internally to free us from this internal curse.

Iniquity is a spiritual nature that is placed on people and passes down onto the children. But, we can be free from it. We can be free from any curse that is in our family. We can break the cycle of passing down from generation to generation.

---

[91] God does not immediately place a curse on someone. First God tries to give a person direction. If they ignore God's direction, He will correct using chastisement. If that doesn't work, then God will rebuke. If that doesn't work, then the sinner becomes cursed.

James 1:15 says:

Then when nature has conceived, it brings forth sin: and sin, when it is finished, brings forth death.

The sin nature is not the sin itself, but the thing inside that causes a person to *want* to sin. It is a nature that "**brings forth sin.**" Of course, everyone has free will and can choose to not listen to that little voice inside crying out for that vice. Just because you have a sin nature, does not mean you have to listen to it. But, you can be free from the sin nature. God can remove that little voice that pushes you toward something that you do not want to do.

Anyone who has known someone who is an alcoholic and goes to AA[92] meetings knows what they say there. People take turns, standing up and say, *"Hello everyone, my name is such-and-such, I am an alcoholic. I haven't had a drink in ten years."* This illustrates my point exactly. Even though the person doesn't drink, the people at the AA meetings acknowledge that the nature is there, the desire to drink is there, that internal longing is there. That is what God can remove. He can free you from the desire for the sin. He can free you from the longing for it. Alcoholics say that *"Once you are an alcoholic, you are always an alcoholic"* even if you do not drink for ten years. When God is done removing the addiction to alcohol, you would say, *"I am not an alcoholic, I am free from it!"*

Jesus' Bruise

The symbols in the Bible have a direct relationship to what

---

[92] AA stands for Alcoholics Anonymous.

they represent. For example, Jesus received bodily damage to take on our bodily ailments. He took on physical "stripes" to give us healing. He took on death to give us life. He was crucified to give us eternal life. Likewise, he took on mental, emotional, and psychological "bruising" to give us freedom from internal iniquity.

We can be free from any sin nature or any mental, emotional, or psychological problem we have simply by asking for it to be taken away. He has already taken it on, we only have to acknowledge the fact that it is already done. Pray in faith believing that He has already done it.

We know that Jesus took on death through the crucifixion and we know that He took on physical "stripes" when He was whipped and scourged by the Roman soldiers. But when did He take on this internal bruising of the soul?

Jesus was "bruised for our iniquity" in the garden of Gethsemane, prior to His capture by the soldiers. But before we get to the garden, let us open up the story at the last supper. There are a few significant things that happen here that affect what happens in the garden. We start out at the tail end of the last supper, reading in John 13:

> 2 And supper being ended, **the devil having now put into the heart of Judas Iscariot, Simon's *son*, to betray Him [Jesus];**

Then Jesus says:

> 18 *"I speak not of you all: I know whom I have chosen: but that the scripture may be fulfilled, he that eateth bread with Me hath lifted up his heel against Me."*
> 21 When Jesus had thus said, He was troubled in spirit, and testified, and said,

> *"Verily, verily, I say unto you, that one of you shall betray Me."*
>
> 25 He then lying on Jesus' breast saith unto him, *"Lord, who is it?"*
>
> 26 Jesus answered, *"He it is, to whom I shall give a sop, when I have dipped it."*
>
> And when He had dipped the sop, He gave *it* to Judas Iscariot, *the son* of Simon.
>
> 27 And after the sop **Satan entered into him.** Then said Jesus unto him, *"That thou doest, do quickly."*
>
> 30 He then having received the sop went immediately out: and it was night.
>
> 31 Therefore, when he was gone out, Jesus said, ***"NOW is the Son of Man glorified, and God is glorified in Him."***

What is happening here at this moment in the last supper is Jesus is giving permission to the Devil to kill Him. Prior to this significant event, the Devil only had limited permission. The Devil was held back. Many times the Pharisees or towns people tried to kill Jesus[being driven by the Devil], but He always "slipped away."[93] Now, Jesus gave the Devil and all his army permission to place their full arsenal of spiritual warfare against Him. He gave His permission for them to torment, to attack, and to destroy Him.

Notice that Jesus says, *"NOW is the Son of Man glorified, and God is glorified in Him."* He was not yet crucified, yet Jesus clearly states that **NOW** it has happened. The fulfillment of Isaiah 53 takes place from this moment until the

---

[93] John 5:13, Luke 14:47, Mark 14:49, John 8:59

moment that Jesus is hanging from the cross and says, *"It is finished."*[94] Many people focus only on the cross. The events that lead up to the crucifixion are significant also. The bruising, the stripes, and the cross are all tied together.

Now, Jesus goes to the garden of Gethsemane to pray. He has an unseen army of darkness piling up misery on His mind, His soul, and every ounce of His being. Matthew 26:36-39 says:

> Then cometh Jesus with them unto a place called Gethsemane, and saith unto the disciples, *"Sit ye here, while I go and pray yonder."*
>
> And He took with him Peter and the two sons of Zebedee, **and began to be sorrowful and very heavy.**
>
> Then saith He unto them, ***"My soul is exceeding sorrowful, even unto death:*** *tarry ye here, and watch with Me."*
>
> And He went a little further, and **fell on His face**, and prayed, saying, *"O my Father, if it be possible, **let this cup pass from Me:** nevertheless not as I will, but as Thou wilt."*

Some people have focused on this statement, *"Let this cup pass from Me"* and said that Jesus did not want to die. They say that the "cup" is the cross. Not so. Jesus had the full weight of all the world's iniquity bearing down on His soul. He was *"exceeding sorrowful, even unto death."* He had great depression, great woe, great anguish, and great misery. So much that He *wanted* to die. He was sorrowful **"unto death!"** When a person gets depression and misery to a certain level, it is not long before they *want* to die.

---

[94] John 19:30

The darkness becomes unbearable for them. Jesus had so much misery due to this great burden of all the world's iniquity that He would *want* to die.

Jesus' physical body was having a hard time handling this deep, deep woe. Jesus the man knew his body would be destroyed, but this burden of misery and anguish was huge! This burden of iniquity was so great that it caused His body to hemorrhage blood. Luke 22:44 says:

> And being in an agony He [Jesus] prayed more earnestly: and **His sweat was as it were great drops of blood** falling down to the ground.

So Jesus did what every Christian should do, He prayed. And what was the answer to His prayer? Luke 22: 41-43 says:

> And He was withdrawn from them about a stone's cast, and kneeled down, and prayed, Saying, *"Father, if Thou be willing, remove this cup from Me: nevertheless not My will, but Thine, be done."* **And there appeared an angel unto Him from heaven, strengthening Him.**

This huge amount of mental anguish was not because He was "afraid" of the cross. The cross is the whole reason He was born. He was slain before the foundation of the world.[95] The misery, the anguish, the bruising of the soul, the bruising of the psyche was nearly more than He could bear so the Father strengthens Him.

Jesus was bruised for our iniquity. Jesus took on this huge internal burden, this huge misery of the soul so that we might be free from any and all iniquity.

---

[95] John 17:24, Hebrews 9:26, 1st Peter 1:20, Revelation 13:8

How to Be Free

Freedom from Iniquity comes quite simply from placing it on the cross. People feel very comfortable asking God to forgive them of their sins, but they never seem to take the next step and ask to be free of the **desire** for that sin.

Remember Romans 13:13-14 says:
> **Let us walk honestly, as in the day; not in rioting and drunkenness, not in chambering and wantonness, not in strife and envying.**
> **But put ye on the Lord Jesus Christ, and make not provision for the flesh, to fulfill the lusts thereof.**

Typically, the Holy Spirit will start to convict you of a sin, especially if it is one that you cannot seem to get away from. To convict simply means to be made to feel guilty. You will feel guilty about doing it, even if you cannot stop doing or thinking about it. What God is doing is pointing it out to you. It is like God saying, *"What are you going to do about this? Do you want me to remove it for you?"*

Now you have to choose. Remember, we always have a choice. Once you finally make that decision that you truly want to be free from the smoking, drinking, cursing, or some other desires, God can remove it. But do not think that you are going to trick God. He knows your heart. He knows when you are truly sincere. He knows when you truly want to be free from that thing.

Once you are truly sincere, then all you have to do is ask. Pray in faith for God to remove that desire. Pray in faith for God to change your nature in that area. He will do it.[96]

Do you have habits that you want to be free from? You may come from a long line of thieves, alcoholics, or gluttons and are sick and tired of it? Be free from this curse. Ask Jesus to come into your heart and free you from this generational curse. He will do it. He has promised it. He will give you a new nature that is free from all of it.

---

[96] The way to pray for freedom from iniquity is the same way you pray for freedom from sickness. In one you are praying for physical bodily healing, in the other you are praying for healing of the soul.

Twelve

ERRORS IN EXTREME

eople sometimes migrate toward two opposite extremes in doctrine. Two examples are found in the doctrines of justification and sanctification. These two doctrines have been around for nearly five-hundred and three-hundred years respectively and have been misused and misinterpreted for just as long.

I will try to give an overview of the two opposite points of view on each and show what the scriptures say. In this essay I am trying to display how people can carry a point out too far and get away from the true Word of God. Even to the point where they will deny portions of the Bible just so they do not have to change their doctrine.

Justification

Justification is a term that sums up the idea that we are made *just* by becoming a true Christian. We are *just* in a legal sense, that is to say that we are made to be on the right side of the law, we are made to be not guilty, or we are made to be righteous by faith in the saving blood of Jesus.

This idea was put forth with great controversy by Martin Luther in the 1520's. He initially called it *sola fide,* meaning "only faith" or "faith alone." He was attacking a system that existed in the Church. During the previous one thousand years of Church history a large system had developed that was based upon *works* being an integral part of the salvation process.

Justified by Works

The argument for works is based on the scriptures found in the second chapter of the epistle of *James*:

14 What *doth it* profit, my brethren, though a man say he hath faith, and have not works? **can faith save him?**

15 If a brother or sister be naked, and destitute of daily food,

16 And one of you say unto them, "*Depart in peace, be ye warmed and filled*"; notwithstanding ye give them not those things which are needful to the body; what *doth it* profit?

17 Even so **faith, if it hath not works, is dead**, being alone.

18 Yea, a man may say, "*Thou has faith, and I have works: shew me thy faith without*

> *thy works, and I will shew thee my faith by my works."*
>
> 21 Was not Abraham our father **justified by works**, when he had offered Isaac his son upon the altar?
>
> 24 **Ye see then how that by works a man is justified, and not by faith only.**
>
> 25 Likewise also was not Rahab the harlot **justified by works**, when she had received the messengers, and had sent *them* out another way?

In the time prior to Martin Luther's challenge to the Church, a believer had to have two things to be forgiven for sin according to Catholic tradition. First, be repentant, guilty, or *sorry* for the sin. Second, the person had to undergo *poena* or temporal punishment because God had been offended. *Poena* is the root of the word *penance*.

These sins, and therefore the penance debt, were additive and people could carry a huge debt burden of penance which must be satisfied before they could enter heaven. Purgatory is a place where people who were dead, yet still had penance to perform, could "work off" their accumulated sin debt. Once the penance debt was satisfied, the person would be let free from purgatory and could enter heaven.

Before a person dies, they could do good works to satisfy some of the penance debt, but once the person dies, there was nothing that could be *done* to satisfy the debt. The only way to satisfy the debt in purgatory was with "time served." Therefore, these penance credits for doing good works came to be termed in the units of reducing time in purgatory. For example, saying the "Our Father" prayer might be worth 2 days off in purgatory.

One nice facet in this system was that people could share. I could do penance for a loved one, living or dead, and work off some of their sin debt. We were all in it together! Likewise, someone very holy, the apostle Paul for example, had more penance *credits* than he needed and therefore could give his excess to others. In 1343, Pope Clement VI decreed that all the excess good works were in a mystical treasury that he had control of called the "treasury of merit."

Good works were set up for people to perform like serving in a crusade, or building a church, for example. If the church to be built was far away, then a person might be able to pay for it to be built as a form of a good work. This idea of buying merits with money soon led to the outright selling of indulgences. Pope Sixtus IV issued a decree in 1476 that said money would deliver souls from purgatory. As if this were not bad enough, the local secular governments pushed the Church into selling more and more indulgences because the princes took as much as two-thirds of the money.

The selling of indulgences became excessive and outrageous. Johann Tetzel, a Dominican friar, was credited with the infamous saying, *"When a penny in the coffer rings, a soul from purgatory springs"* which typifies how bad it became. Tetzel said that as soon as the coin hit the bottom of the collection box, the soul trapped in purgatory was released.

Martin Luther became so upset with the selling of indulgences that he wrote an open letter to the princes complaining about the status of the Church and asking them to help in its reform. It was called the *95 Theses*, and in it he says, *"Why does not the Pope liberate everyone from purgatory for the sake of love (a most holy thing) or for the supreme necessity of their souls?"* He hit the nail on the head, by basically saying, *"What is more important: a person's soul or erecting a new building? If the Pope has control over all these excess good works, why doesn't he use* *them to save souls? Why doesn't he use them to free <u>everyone</u> from purgatory?"*

So, this is one end of the extreme, that works are an integral part of the salvation process. Of course, if there is some work that we could do to be saved then Jesus did not have to come. Yet, they were not saying that exactly. They were saying that we needed BOTH the blood of Jesus and works to enter into heaven. But that is still Biblically incorrect.

Justified by Faith

In any case, let us look at the opposite end of the extreme. Martin Luther's new doctrine was that we are saved by faith ALONE. Luther based much of his doctrine on the book of Romans:

> For therein is the righteousness of God revealed from faith to faith: as it is written, **The just shall live by faith.**(1:17)

> Therefore we conclude that a man is **justified by faith** without the deeds of the law. (3:28)

> For if Abraham were justified by works, he hath *whereof* to glory; but not before God. For what saith the scripture? **Abraham believed God**, and it was counted unto him for righteousness. (4:2-3)

> Therefore being **justified by faith**, we have peace with God through our Lord Jesus Christ (5:1)

Works did not matter one little bit to Luther. Now, one of the consequences of any new doctrine is that many people interpret that doctrine incorrectly by taking it to an extreme. When Luther said that we are saved by faith *alone* and works do not matter, he had to deal with scriptures that speak on works, in particular, the book of *James* that we first listed. What was Luther's solution? He basically said that those scriptures were no good! In fact, Luther wanted parts of the Bible removed, reinterpreted, or at least de-emphasized. Luther altered one of his most used scriptures. In Romans 1:17, it says, "...The just shall live by faith." Luther changed it to say, "...The just shall live by faith **alone**."

We can look at this idea of discrediting portions of the Bible in detail by looking at Martin Luther's *Preface to the German Translation of the New Testament*, written in 1522. Here are a few quotes:

> For the gospel does not expressly demand works of our own by which we become righteous and are saved; indeed it condemns such works.

> ...so that one sees on every hand that the gospel is not a book of law, but really a preaching of the benefits of Christ, shown to us and given to us for our own possession, if we believe. But Moses, in his books, drives, compels, threatens, strikes, and rebukes terribly, for he is a law giver and driver.

Luther then asks, "Which are the true and noblest books of the New Testament?" He goes on to tell which books are his favorites. And why are these his favorites? Because they emphasis Jesus' preaching and not His miracles, not His works.

> If I had to do without one or the other –
> either the works or the preaching of Christ – I
> would rather do without the works than without
> His preaching. For the works do not help me,
> but His words give life…

He goes on dramatically to totally discredit the book of *James*. Why? Because this book so heavily speaks on works:

> Therefore, **St. James epistle is really an epistle of straw**, compared to these others, for it has nothing of the nature of the gospel about it.

Now, do not think I am trying to bash Luther or present day Lutherans for that matter. I am only holding him up because I feel if this "great man of God" could make this huge mistake, we ought to learn from it and not do the same.

But let me tell you how serious this was. In Germany, the Bible was mostly only available in Latin, and perhaps Greek and Hebrew. Of course there were a few others, the Czech Bible and Wycliffe's English Bible for example, but those would have been little help to a German. The Gutenberg press had only been developed about 80 years prior. Bibles were just not available to people, much less in a common local language that people could read.

So here comes Luther. He does a wonderful and much needed work of translating a Latin New Testament into German for the people, but then what does he tack onto the front of it? His introduction, where he discredits the parts of the Bible that he does not like. Then this Bible is printed and is read. Mind you, many who read it will be reading a Bible for the first time ever in their lives and they start out on page one with a statement that part of this book is no good.

This idea sounds extreme, but you can still hear it today in a different form. People argue the Bible and say, "*My scripture is better than your scripture.*" Or they say, "*You keep your scripture, and I'll keep my scripture.*" As if one scripture trumps another. The fact of the matter is that ALL scripture must be in agreement. If your doctrine has one scripture in conflict with another then it is *your* doctrine that is incorrect, NOT the scripture.

Isaiah 28:10 says:
> For precept must be upon precept, precept upon precept; line upon line, line upon line; here a little, and there a little...

This verse means that every line of the Word of God must be in agreement. Precept must be upon precept. Every precept must be in agreement. Every line must be in agreement. If not then your doctrine is wrong, not the Bible.

Extreme Results

Another result of this new doctrine of justification was that it was used as an excuse for not helping others. The idea was that if we are saved by faith *alone* then we do not need to do good works anymore. Many people stopped. They stopped giving to charity, stopped helping out at orphanages, stopped doing anything voluntary. "*Why should I do anything extra,*" they thought, "*I do not need to work off any penance, I am already saved!*"

Balthasar Hubmaier testified of this in his 1527 letter to the Lord Margrave of Brandenburg titled *On Free Will*. He says, "*Indeed, I have heard from many people that for a long time they have not prayed, nor fasted, nor given alms because their priests tell how their works are of no avail before God and therefore they at once let them go."* (Williams, 115)

Of course they were missing the point. In fact, they were missing the point even before the point was made. You see, they believed that works saved. So, the only reason they did the works was because they were selfish and did not want to go to Hell. Again, they were trying to buy their way into heaven.

So what is the right answer? We do works because it is our nature in us driving us to do them. Not in our old sinful nature, but in the new nature that God gives us. Ephesians 2:8-10 puts the whole controversy between faith and works in perfect balance. It says:

> For it is **by grace you have been saved**, through faith—and this not from yourselves, it is the gift of God— not by works, so that no one can boast.
> For we are God's workmanship, **created in Christ Jesus to do good works**, which God prepared in advance for us to do.

We are saved by God's grace. Salvation is what He does for us. Faith is the channel that we use to connect to God. And *after* we are saved, good works are what we do for Him. If we do not do good works, then our faith is dead. The good works do not save us, but they are a **result** of being saved. Inside of you, in your *spirit*, you are changed to a person who *wants* to perform good works. You have a new nature. If you do not want to do them, if there is not something in your inner core being that wants to do good works, then you have not Jesus inside.[97]

---

[97] If you want a further explanation on this point, See the essay *Sin and Faith*.

Sanctification

Sanctification was a doctrine that originated shortly after Martin Luther's justification. It was discussed by Martin Bucer among others but was called "second justification" or "double justification" in the 1500's. The ideas on sanctification that these reformers had were not complete at this time.

John Wesley fully developed the idea of sanctification in the 1740's. It was also called "Christian perfection," "holiness of heart," or "life holiness" in addition to "sanctification." Wesley was an Anglican clergyman who was an early leader in the Methodist movement.

Sanctification means "to set apart for special use or purpose," that is, to make holy or sacred. It comes from the Latin word *sanctus* which translates to "holy." So, the idea is that our actual external behavior should be holy and pure if we are Christians. Wesley realized that the outward behavior comes directly from the inner condition or nature of a person and therefore, no matter how hard we try to clean up our lives on our own, we will always return back to sin as long as we have a sin nature inside of us. His solution was prayer and fasting to beg for God to change our nature. To beg God to sanctify us. He held large and small tent meetings where people would pray for as long as it took until the Holy Spirit would fall. After the Spirit fell, people were changed. They became holy. They stopped all their sinful habits and dressed properly. They did not stop sinning because they were concerned of what others would think, but because they were changed *inside*.[98]

---

[98] The scriptures Romans 12:9-21 and 1st Thessalonians 4:1-12 were used heavily by Wesley and later Methodists to support his doctrine of sanctification.

"Wesley insisted that in this life, the Christian could come to a state where the love of God, or perfect love, reigned supreme in a person's heart. By the power of God's sanctifying grace and attention upon the means of grace, a Christian could be cleansed of the corrupting influence of original sin in this life."[99] Now there are two general ideas on how sanctification works. For Wesley and for Methodists in general, *sanctification* is a life-long process, but for Holiness Wesleyans, entire sanctification comes in an instantaneous transformation.[100]

Legalism

Now the problem comes in when the churches, who believe in Wesley's holiness doctrine, tried to *enforce* holiness. See they apparently did not want to wait for God to change the hearts of the people. Their idea was that they could legislate holiness or force people to be holy through rules.

For example, some churches station a deacon at the entrance of the church. The deacon would not let anyone in who is not dressed to the church standards. People who are known to have immoral behavior are prevented from entering. This is still practiced today in some churches.

---

[99] See en.wikipedia.org, John Wesley

[100] In the life-long process sanctification, God points out a sin to a person. That person willfully gives up that sin and asks God to clean them and remove it. At that point God removes the sin nature for that one sin. This process continues until death.
  In the instantaneous sanctification, the person's sin nature is not instantaneously removed, but God's shed blood covers all of the person's sin and thus instantaneously covers them, making the person sanctified. In my explanation, instantaneous sanctification is the same thing as grace and therefore is not sanctification at all.

There are other groups that practice shunning. Members of the church are not allowed to see or talk to someone who is *shunned* by the church for unholy behavior. They say that if you do not dress or act a certain way, then you are out. The women do not wear wedding rings. Women wear long hair and long skirts. Absolutely no makeup is allowed. The men have to wear long sleeves and cannot roll them up.

Is this starting to sound familiar yet? Think of the Pharisees. They were awful holy on the outside, but inside full of dead men's bones. Some of them at least.

Now, I can appreciate any stance on holiness. I am all for it. But do it the right way. Let God change your spirit nature so that you *want* to be holy. Not being holy so that you can fit into some man-made group. Do not be a hypocrite. Do not try to *look* holy while your inside is still rotten. Let the Holy Spirit change your nature and be clean inside and out.

Now, I do not want that to be misunderstood. Again, I am all for holiness and a Christian dressing and acting like a Christian. A Christian should be recognized as being different from the world in their dress and actions. And remember, when we are going to church, we are going to meet God. We should dress and act respectful and reverent. I do not have a problem with a church making sure that people are dressed respectful in the house of God, but do not make the mistake of thinking that you are sanctifying them by forcing them to change their style of dress.

Grace

The opposite extreme is when people latch onto grace. They believe that external actions do not matter at all. They are saved by God's grace so they can do whatever they want.

"Jesus' blood covers all sin, so I can sin all I want," they think.

"I don't have to be holy because I can just confess my sins every Sunday and start out with a new, clean slate," they say.

These people are in the opposite extreme and are surely lost. Romans 6:15 says, "What then? Shall we sin because we are not under law but under grace? Certainly not!"

Yes, we are saved by the grace of God. But in the salvation process, God will change your nature so that you do not *want* to sin. You will *want* to be holy. You will have a new nature after you are converted.

Conclusion

So you have seen that any doctrine can be taken to extremes. But you have also seen that when it goes to extreme, it walks away from the Word. Even the chosen messengers of God have made mistakes and walked away from the Word. Take this as a lesson. Never be too proud to say that you are wrong. If your doctrine conflicts with the Word of God then it is your doctrine that is wrong, not the Word.

Thirteen

THE WILL

 n this essay I wish to speak on the *exact* point at which grace and holiness rub, so you might know why these two ideas *seem* to conflict. Also, we will discuss how **the sacrifice of the will** leads to the baptism of the Holy Ghost.[101]

Salvation is sometimes presented as a three-step process called justification, sanctification, and the baptism of the Holy Ghost.[102]

First, we accept Jesus as our Lord and savior and make a public declaration of our faith. That is justification. Second, the

---

[101] This position, that the sacrifice of the will leads to the baptism of the Holy Ghost, is my opinion based on personal experience and observation.

[102] Sometimes the salvation process is described as four, five or more steps.

Holy Spirit starts convicting us of our sin and we start to clean up our lives. As we detailed in *Iniquity*, the Holy Spirit will make us aware of a sin or a sin nature. If we choose to give it up, the Holy Spirit can help us by removing the desire for the sin. That is sanctification. Finally, we come to a place where the Holy Spirit enters in and indwells the believer. This is the indwelling. Sounds easy and clear-cut, right? Wrong.

On the surface this may sound simple but if we pull on the strings a little, the sweater will start to unravel. Since it is described as a three-step process, we naturally think the first step is first and second step is second. But in reality, it is much more complex. We can find people who are justified without being sanctified. We can find people who live a holy and sanctified life without being justified, and people who *claim* to have the Holy Ghost who are neither justified nor sanctified.

People who are justified without being sanctified are easy enough to find. They gave their hearts to Jesus and they are standing on His Word to save them, yet they are still living in their sins. Sometimes people are sanctified bodily, meaning that they do not actually perform sins, but they are still carnally-minded. They are not sanctified in their soul. We can also find people who live a holy and sanctified life but are not justified. People who could not live a more holy life, yet have never given their lives to Jesus. There is such a variety out there that we cannot line up our three-step process neatly. It is not a cookbook.

Now, what about the baptism of the Holy Spirit? If we have to be sanctified first, how can we ever receive it? We said, *"clean the inside of the cup first before we drink out of it."*[103] Yet we also said that the Holy Spirit would remove the sin nature. So which comes first?

---

[103] Matthew 23:24-28

If we think even deeper, we can raise even more questions. How can we ever receive the indwelling if we are not truly and completely free of all sin? If we are not truly and completely free of all sin, how can we be sanctified? I mean, we are always *thinking* something that could be considered unbelief. How can the Holy Ghost come if the cup is constantly being dirtied over and over? The answer is grace.

Sanctification and Grace

Sanctification is a process where the Holy Spirit convicts a person of sin and that person can pray for the Holy Spirit to not only forgive them of the sin, but also remove the sin nature. This can and does happen *before* the person receives the indwelling of the Holy Spirit. The Holy Spirit CAN and DOES speak to you before you have the indwelling. Additionally, This process can also happen *after* the person receives the indwelling.

Remember that the human being is composed of three parts: a spirit, a soul, and a body.[104] We must strive to be sanctified in all three. When we become justified, we receive the gift of righteousness by Jesus' blood. There is a change that takes place inside of us. When we become indwelt, the Holy Spirit takes up permanent residence inside of us, with our own spirit. There is a second more dramatic change that takes place inside of us.

The processes of sanctification for the soul (the mind) and the body are separate from the spirit and, in a way, each other. Of course, our external actions are controlled to a degree by our mind

---

[104] 1st Thessalonians 5:23

and spirit, therefore, if we sanctify the internal, the external will also become sanctified because we will not *want* to sin.[105]

Can a person ever be completely and totally sanctified in their actions and thoughts while on earth? I am not sure at this time, but there are some who hold this doctrine and they call it *glorification*. Others say we can only reach this glorified state in heaven. So, let us assume that we cannot reach this state of perfection. Then how can we receive the indwelling of the Holy Spirit when we are never wholly sanctified? This is exactly where grace steps in. Romans 6:14 says:

> For sin shall not have dominion over you,
> for you are not under law but under grace.

John 1:17 says:

> For the law was given through Moses,
> but grace and truth came through Jesus
> Christ.

And Romans 5:17, 20-21 says:

> For if by the one man's offense death
> reigned through the one, much more those
> who receive abundance of grace and of the
> gift of righteousness will reign in life through
> the One, Jesus Christ.
> Moreover the law entered that the
> offense might abound.
> **But where sin abounded, grace
> abounded much more, so that as sin
> reigned in death, even so grace might
> reign through righteousness to eternal
> life through Jesus Christ** our Lord.

When we are in this state of grace, we are in a state where when God looks down at us, he does not see our sins but only the

---

[105] This was the whole point of the Sin and Faith essay.

blood of Jesus. We are covered by his blood. But never sin willfully. God forbid. We want to be as good as we can and try to be perfect as we can. But whatever sins we still perform or think will be covered by Jesus' blood.

Grace

Sanctification is a continual process that is always happening for every believer. While this process of sanctification is happening, grace covers the "unconvicted" sin. Let me explain how this works.

Let us say that a person is a new Christian and has much sin and tendencies toward sin. The Lord will come to that person and bless them greatly, even though they are still sinning. they are babes in Christ, so there is much grace given.

After a while the Lord will start to convict the person of some sin. Maybe even just one sinful behavior. Until the person recognizes this sin and gives it up to God, the Spirit of God will start to slowly pull away. If the person does not repent of the sin, after a time the Lord will pull His grace away and tribulations will occur.

Hopefully, the person eventually gets the message and repents of that sin and puts it on the cross. The Holy Spirit re-establishes His blessing and relationship with the person and the grace covers all the remaining sins. Then the process starts again.

Of course, the problems really start when God is calling for a person to give up a sin and the person holds onto it. God will only take you as far as you are willing to go and when a person refuses to give up a sin it blocks the spiritual progress of that person and they stagnate.[106]

The Will

The process of sanctification could also be viewed as the process of giving the world up to God, piece by piece. We are sacrificing worldly things that we like to do or think about. For example, people may be addicted to gambling, but usually it starts because they like it. We know we shouldn't, it is against God's Word, but it is hard to tear away from that thing because we like it. But, in order to become more righteous, we give it up. Now the ultimate and usually the last thing that people give up is their own will.

The will is the hardest thing to lose. To lose your own choice of the things you do, where you go, and what you want to do with your life. Yet, to receive the indwelling, I believe, you **must** give up your will.[107]

I would like to use the life of Rees Howells to illustrate this point. Rees was a person called to intercessory prayer during the Welsh revival in the 1890's. Let me first tell you about Rees Howells' conversion. He had given his life to Jesus and Jesus took the place of everything he had, his home, wife and children, and the world (Grubb 29). He was happy about this and went on living, but trying to do things for the kingdom of God. This was

---

[106] Some people say that you are backslidden if you are not moving forward. Even staying in the same place is like going backwards because you are supposed to move forward.

[107] This opinion is based on my own personal experience.

the first step, justification. He gave his life to Jesus. He made a confession of faith.

Then one day, the Holy Spirit came calling and asked Rees for all those things that he promised to give to God. The Holy Spirit came and asked for full possession. The Holy Spirit wanted Rees to become sanctified. Rees said:

> The Holy Ghost appeared to me and I knew him to be the One who had spoken to me…
>
> It never dawned on me before that the Holy Ghost…must come and dwell in flesh and blood…
>
> I had only thought of Him as an influence coming on meetings, and that was what most of us in the revival thought. [108]
>
> I had never seen that He must live in bodies, as the savior lived in His on earth (39).

Then the Holy Spirit spoke to Rees. God said:

> I *dwell* in the *cleansed* temple of the believer. *I am a person.*
>
> I am God, and I am come to ask you to give your body to Me that I may work through it.
>
> I need a body for My temple, but it must belong to Me without reserve, for two persons with different wills can never live in the same body.
>
> Will you give Me yours? But if I come in, I come as God, and *you must go out.*
>
> I shall not mix Myself with yourself. (40)

---

[108] Remember the difference between being filled with the Holy Spirit and the indwelling of the Holy Spirit. Rees had many experiences with the Holy Spirit, but had never received the person of God. The *"influence coming on meetings"* was the filling of the Holy Spirit.

Rees battled with his decision for a long time. He cried for days. He realized what it was he was giving up. God will not trick you into giving up something. God lets you know exactly what he is asking for. He will point out an exact sin and say, "*We cannot move forward one more step in your life as a Christian because this one sin right here is blocking your path.*" It would seem easy to give things up, but in reality it can be very hard. Things that we have done all our lives, things that seem normal to us, can be a road block to God.

Rees had already given up most of these things, now God was asking Rees to give up his WILL. But, your will IS your whole life! Your will is what you want to do. Your will is making decisions for yourself. Rees was living his life for God, he was choosing God's ways, but now God wanting something more. God was not satisfied with him choosing anymore, God wanted full possession. God wanted to make the decisions.

This was a great struggle. God was asking Rees to die as a person. Who could make a decision like that in a moment? He said:

> *Why does a man struggle when death comes, if it is easy to die?*
> *I intended to do it, but oh, the cost! How I wished I had never seen it!* (40)

Remember that in Matthew 16:25, Jesus says:

> *For whosoever will save his life shall lose it: and whosoever will lose his life for My sake shall find it.*

Rees started to come around. He said:

> *He [the Holy Spirit] had only come to take what I had already promised...*

264

> *Since He died for me, **I had to die for Him**, and I knew that this new life was His and not mine…*
>
> *I saw that only the Holy Ghost in me could live like the savior.*
>
> *Everything He told me appealed to me; it was only a question of the loss…*
>
> *The Holy Spirit went on… **exposing the root of my nature which was self…***
>
> *He put His finger on each part of my self-life, and I had to decide…*
>
> ***He could never take a thing away until I gave my consent.***
>
> *Then the morning I gave it, some purging took place…*
>
> *It was not saying I was purged and the thing still having a hold on me: no, **it was a breaking, and the Holy Ghost taking control.*** (41)

The Holy Spirit was not yet indwelling Rees, but speaking to him and sanctifying him. The Holy Spirit will point out where you are failing and if you are *willing* to give it to the Lord, then He will remove your desire for it. Remember, you always have a choice. This process can take years for some people. For others it can be quick. It all depends upon the individual.

Jesus said, *"Verily, verily, I say unto you, Except a corn of wheat fall into the ground and die, it abideth alone: but if it die, it bringeth forth much fruit."* (John 12:24)

No wonder Jesus said it was so difficult for a rich man to enter; they have so much to give up. Not that they have so many physical things to give up, but they have so much internal desire for those physical things. They have placed so many physical things at a higher priority than God. Of course, there certainly are rich people who place God first, but Jesus was only saying that this is a difficult thing to do.

Isaiah recounts a similar experience with God. He says:
> Then said I, "*Woe is me! for I am undone; because I am a man of unclean lips, and I dwell in the midst of a people of unclean lips: for mine eyes have seen the King, the LORD of hosts.*"
> Then flew one of the seraphims unto me, having a live coal in his hand, *which* he had taken with the tongs from off the altar:
> And he laid *it* upon my mouth, and said, "*Lo, this hath touched thy lips; and thine iniquity is taken away, and thy sin purged.*"[109]

Is this all really necessary? Yes. Romans 12:1 says:
> I beseech you therefore, brethren, by the mercies of God, that ye **present your bodies a living sacrifice, holy, acceptable unto God,** *which is* **your reasonable service.**

And Colossians 3:2-3 says:
> **Set your affection on things above**, not on things on the earth.
> **For ye are dead, and your life is hid with Christ in God.**

And Romans 6:3-4 says:
> Know ye not, that so many of us as were baptized into Jesus Christ were baptized into His death?
> **Therefore we are buried with Him by baptism into death:** that like as Christ was raised up from the dead by the glory of the

---

[109] See Isaiah 6:5-7.

Father, even so we also should walk in
newness of life.

Finally, 1st Corinthians 6:19-20 says:

What? know ye not that your body is the
temple of the Holy Ghost *which is* in you,
which ye have of God, and **ye are not your
own?**

For **ye are bought with a price**: therefore
glorify God in your body, and in your spirit,
which are God's.

Rees continues in the sanctification process for years. He
said:

*...I had always had fear of the searchings
of the Holy Spirit....*

*People may think they have no fear when
really they have never been tested.*

*I had to be pulled through inch by inch; it
was the process of sanctification,* **when the
self-nature and all its lusts had to be
exchanged for the divine nature**... (138)

Romans 6:6 says:

Knowing this, that **our old man is
crucified with *Him***, that the body of sin
might be destroyed, that henceforth we
should not serve sin.

Did you catch that? We are "**crucified with Him.**" Our sin
nature, the old self that we are, must die. It must be crucified. We
must die out to all our old ways, and all our old desires. Our *self*
must die in order to be replaced with the new self, the Holy Spirit.

Remember, we also have grace working in conjunction. As
long as we are striving toward the goal, grace will cover our
shortcomings. Continue to press toward the goal. Let the Holy

Spirit work with you. Grace will cover you along your path.
Philippians 3:8-11 says:

> Yea doubtless, and I count all things but
> loss for the excellency of the knowledge of
> **Christ Jesus my Lord: for whom I have**
> **suffered the loss of ALL things**, and do
> count them but dung, that I may win Christ,
>
> And be found in Him, not having mine
> own righteousness, which is of the law, but
> that which is through the faith of Christ, the
> righteousness which is of God by faith:
>
> That I may know Him, and the power of
> His resurrection, and **the fellowship of His**
> **sufferings, being made conformable**
> **unto His death;**
>
> If by any means I might attain unto the
> resurrection of the dead.

The Indwelling comes

Now remember, we might not ever reach a point where we
are completely sanctified in actions and thoughts. We have God's
grace as a covering. But after you give up **your will**, the Holy
Spirit will enter.

Rees Howells received the indwelling in a group setting
similar to Pentecost. It was at a Bible College in England during
the First World War. Because of the Nazi bombing, there were no
classes. Instead the students and faculty would gather to pray.

After a time, they were all in one accord, just like at Pentecost. He says:

An awesome sense of nearness began to steal over the whole College. There was a solemn expectancy...

God was there; yet we were still waiting for Him to come. And in the days that followed, **He came.**

*...gradually the **Person** of the Holy Ghost filled all out thoughts, His presence filled all the place, and His light seemed to penetrate all the hidden recesses of our hearts.*

...We felt the Holy Spirit had been a real Person to us before; as far as we knew we had received Him...

But now the revelation of His Person was so tremendous that all our previous experiences seemed as nothing.

...He made Himself so real to our spiritual eyes that it was a 'face to face' experience. And when we saw Him we knew we had never really seen Him before.

...it was not so much sin we saw as self. We saw pride and self-motives underlying everything we had ever done.

He showed us, **"there is all the difference in the world between your surrendered life in My hands, and Me living My life in your body"**

He made it clear that He was not asking for service, but for sacrifice...

How much there was in us that still wanted to live our own lives!...

*One by one **our wills were broken**; we yielded on His own unconditional terms.*

*To one by one there came **this glorious realization: He had entered!**[110] (258-62)*

After they received the indwelling, they were completely different people. All things became new and different for them. Sure, they were already "saved" or "born again," many had given their lives to Jesus decades before. They had dealings with the Holy Spirit before. His "influence had come on the meetings," as Rees put it. But now there was a completely different change that occurred! They were spiritually quickened. They were given new eyes and everything they saw was changed. Even the Bible was new.

Some might say, *"Hey! How come my pastor never told me that I would have to sacrifice? He only tells me about all the good blessings coming my way!"* I cannot answer that question, but Galatians 2:20 says:

> **I am crucified with Christ**: nevertheless I live; **yet not I, but Christ liveth in me**: and the life which I now live in the flesh I live by the faith of the Son of God, who loved me, and gave Himself for me.

And 2nd Corinthians 4:10 says:

> Always bearing about in the body the dying of the Lord Jesus, that the life also of Jesus might be made manifest in our body.

---

[110] Rees' "glorious realization" is the same revelation knowledge that I have mentioned in previous essays.

My Experience

I personally identified with Rees Howells' experience because it was similar to my own. I went through a process of sanctification that also lasted many years. Not saying that it has to take that long, I believe it could take a moment. In any case, I came to a place where the Holy Spirit asked me for *my* will. Do not think that God tricked me into giving it up. God lets you know exactly what you are giving up and the full consequences of your decision. I labored for a long time, but finally I sincerely confessed to God, "*It is all yours, Lord.*" Now, God knows when you are sincere. He knows when you truly mean what you say.

I felt the Fire of God fall on me like never before and the spiritual revelation struck my heart, my innermost being and I KNEW that I was saved, I was indwelled, that I was sealed. The spiritual experience was the same as other times that the Holy Spirit fell on me. The fire was the same. But this time the wind was present also. This time a *spiritual revelation* accompanied the fire. This time, I KNEW that I was saved deep, deep down in my Spirit. This time, I KNEW that I was indwelt.

Then, all of a sudden a misery came on me. I couldn't understand it. "*I thought I was supposed to feel joy?*" I had a tremendous misery and a burden for all the unsaved. Yes, I knew I was saved, but there was *so many* who did not even know the Truth. I felt like my mind and spirit were flying over the entire planet, seeing all the unsaved who didn't seem to even have a chance. My soul was wailing for them! I couldn't understand why I felt this anguish on this happiest of days.

The following day, I was praying and asking God why my experience was so peculiar and what did it mean. I asked Him why I had felt this anguish and misery in my spirit.

He told me to read Ezekiel 9:4. In this verse, God is speaking to an angel. It says:

> And the LORD said unto him [the angel], *"Go through the midst of the city, through the midst of Jerusalem, and **set a mark upon the foreheads of the men that sigh and that cry for all the abominations** that be done in the midst thereof."*

After this event all things became new. I opened the Bible and it was like a new and completely different book. There were things that I had read many times before that I had never really understood. Of course, I thought I understood them, but I was wrong. Now, they were so simple and obvious to me. Now, I saw the true meaning. There is *so much* of the Bible that we cannot even start to understand until we have received the indwelling of the Holy Spirit.

My life was a new life. The Bible was a new Bible. I saw God moving everywhere. I saw the Devil moving everywhere too. It all became so plain to me. It was as if a cloak had been removed from my eyes and the *real* world had been revealed. All the workings behind the scenes were shown for what they really were. I saw Satan's influence on people and likewise, I saw how God was working through people.

Little subtle things changed in me that I could not even see. People would come to me and say, *"You seem different somehow..."* I could not say exactly how my behavior had changed. I had been trying to live a Christian life before this point. Yet, there *was* a change that they saw. It was not necessarily in behavior, but in nature. I was converted from the inside out. I was converted. I was changed.

To truly receive the indwelling, I believe, you must give up your will. I know this is a hard saying. But, you must crucify your old self on the cross with Jesus.[111] And is that so difficult? I mean, are you ready to sacrifice eternity for those high-heeled shoes, video games, and cigarettes? You will be trading in that old junk for magnificent joy and glory.

Once you submit your will to God and He changes you, He converts you, you will never be the same. You will have eternal security, and you will be eternally changed. Your nature will be converted so that you will not desire that old junk. You will have no desire for it. You will be changed from the inside out. You will still have battles; they never end until the day you die.[112] But you will no longer be battling for eternal life. You will have salvation as a possession! Amen.

---

[111] Obviously, I do not mean to literally crucify yourself, but that we crucify our WILL. We sacrifice or give up our will, our desires, and our wants and replace those with God's will. Paul said that we should have "the mind of Christ" (1st Corinthians 2:16) and in order to have His mind, we must sacrifice, crucify, and give up our own mind.

[112] In fact, the battles get harder and harder, but in another way they get easier. More on this in the next book.

END

This is the area of most books where the author describes himself. I am very reluctant to say anything about myself because this book really has nothing to do with me. Additionally, I find it difficult to describe a person accurately in only a few sentences. I find that when most people who write books describe details about themselves they list where they went to college, how many and of what type of degrees they have, how many books they have written, to what societies they belong, blah, blah, blah, some endless list of accomplishments as if these really describe a person.

But, when we look at what the people of the Bible did, the people who God chose, we see a different pattern. Carpenters, tent-makers, doctors, tax collectors, fishermen, housewives, farmers and outdoors-men were the chosen of God. Regular people were chosen to bring a message to the people. And many of them were not very polite. John the Baptist screamed at people, wore weird clothes, and ate bugs!

In the cases where God chose a professionally trained man, God first had to break him down, before he was built back up. Moses was highly educated for 40 years in Egypt, but God left him in the desert for 40 additional years to get Pharaoh's education out of him so he could finally be used.

Of course, there is nothing wrong with formal training as long as a person first has the Holy Spirit. There is a famous old saying that sums up this sentiment. It goes, *"Some people like to read their Bible in Hebrew, some people like to read their Bible in Greek, but I like to read my Bible in the Holy Spirit."* And that sound right to me.

REFERENCES

On This Rock
McGrath, Alister, *Reformation Thought*, Blackwell Publishing, Malden, Mass., 1999

Church Order
Wigglesworth, Smith, *Ever Increasing Faith*, Gospel Publishing House, Springfield, Missouri, 1924

Cycles
The Franklin Institute weather website can be found at www.fi.edu/weather/data2/index.html.

Hagin, Kenneth E., *The Believer's Authority*, RHEMA Bible Church, Tulsa, OK, 1986

God in a Man
Green, Pearry, *Acts of the Prophet*, Tucson Tabernacle Books, Tucson, AZ, 1975

References (continued)

Being Filled
> Wigglesworth, Smith, *On The Holy Spirit*, Whitaker House, New Kensington, PA, 1998

> Wigglesworth, Smith, *Smith Wigglesworth: The Complete Collection of His Life Teachings*, Wilmington Group, Ft. Lauderdale, FL, 1996

Errors in Extreme
> Williams, George Hunston, Editor, *Spiritual and Anabaptist Writers,* The Westminster Press, Philadelphia, PA, 1957

The Will
> Grubb, Norman, *Rees Howells: Intercessor,* CLC Publications, Fort Washington, PA, 1952

ADDITIONAL READING

The Indwelling
Branham, William, *What Is The Holy Ghost?*, 16 Dec 1959, www.branham.org

Branham, William, *What Was The Holy Ghost Given For?*, 17 Dec 1959, www.branham.org

Wigglesworth, Smith, *On The Holy Spirit*, Whitaker House, New Kensington, PA, 1998

Receiving Healing
Bosworth, F. F., *Christ the Healer*, Baker Book House Co., Grand Rapids, Michigan, 1924

Wigglesworth, Smith, *Ever Increasing Faith*, Gospel Publishing House, Springfield, Missouri, 1924

Wigglesworth, Smith, *On Healing*, Whitaker House, New Kensington, PA, 1999

On This Rock
Bromiley, G. W., Editor, *Zwingli and Bullinger*, The Westminster Press, Philadelphia, 1953

Additional Reading (continued)

On This Rock (continued)

Dillenberger, John, Editor, *Martin Luther: Selections from his Writing,* Anchor Books, New York,1962

Dolan, John P., Editor, *The Essential Erasmus*, Meridian, New York, 1983

Hillerbrand, Hans, Editor, *The Protestant Reformation*, Harper Torchbooks, New York, 1968

Church Order
Branham, William, *Church Order*, 26 Dec 1963, www.branham.org

God in a Man
Branham, William, *The Unveiling of God*, 14 June 1964, www.branham.org